PASTORAL LETTERS
TO THE
FAR EAST

PASTORAL LETTERS TO THE FAR EAST

He that goeth forth and weepeth,
bearing precious seed, shall
doubtless come again with rejoicing,
bringing his sheaves with him.
PSALM 126:6

COMPILED BY

SIE SIOK HUI

THE PUBLISHING TRUST
CHURCH ROAD, TYLERS GREEN, PENN, BUCKINGHAMSHIRE.

Printed and Published by
John Metcalfe Publishing Trust
Church Road, Tylers Green,
Penn, Buckinghamshire

—

Distributed by Trust Representatives
and Agents world-wide

In the Far East

Bethany, Orchard Point P.O. Box 0373
Singapore 912313

—

First Published 1997

—

ISBN 1 870039 74 2

—

CONTENTS

INTRODUCTION

Introduction

'HOW beautiful upon the mountains are the feet of him that bringeth good tidings, that publisheth peace; that bringeth good tidings of good, that publisheth salvation; that saith unto Zion, Thy God reigneth!'

Who would behold, let alone admire the feet of such sent messengers? Those who are in distress, who mourn for their poverty; who know they have no righteousness whatsoever, who know they are far removed from the presence of God and cannot please him. Deep in their soul, they feel their condemnation, know their infinite distance from God, who feel the wrath of God revealed from heaven in their consciousness; who were born in sin, who were conceived in iniquity, whose will is in bondage, who sin and sin continually, locked in the power of the authority of darkness.

Yet who could understand one in such a wretched state, and speak to them of salvation bringing hope to them that have no hope, save the chosen vessels of mercy, called of God, prepared and sent by his everlasting commandments to preach such glad tidings to his poor and needy people.

To such as us, who sat in darkness, and in the region and shadow of death, the enduring mercy of our God was made manifest. To us, the voice of the multitude of the heavenly host, 'Glory to God in the highest, and on earth peace, good will toward men', sounding forth, was heard when he sent forth his faithful servant, Mr. John Metcalfe, an able minister of the new testament, to preach the gospel of peace unto us from the twelfth month, 1984, to the 14th of the first month, 1985.

In our solitary ways, we had walked, each feeling within us the preparatory work of one crying in the wilderness of our souls, crying, 'All flesh is grass, and all the goodliness thereof is as the flower of the field: the grass withereth, the flower fadeth: because the spirit of the LORD bloweth upon it: surely the people is grass. The grass withereth, the flower fadeth: but the word of our God shall stand for ever', Isaiah 40:6-8.

'As it is written in the book of the words of Esaias the prophet, saying, The voice of one crying in the wilderness, Prepare ye the way of the Lord, make his paths straight. Every valley shall be filled, and every mountain and hill shall be brought low; and the crooked shall be made straight, and the rough ways shall be made smooth; and all flesh shall see the salvation of God', Luke 3:4-6.

Each was brought low; each walked through the valley of Baca; each came weeping. And in the great mercies of

God each was delivered out of deep soul distress, 'and he led them forth by the right way, that they might go to a city of habitation', Ps. 107:7.

When the Lord's servant, Mr. John Metcalfe, came unto us, we heard the truth of the gospel as we had never heard it before. It was not 'just believing Jesus'; 'letting Jesus into your heart'; 'surrendering your life to God', or any suchlike thing. It was a gospel that was definitive, declaring the Person of Christ; his pre-existence; his deity; his eternal Sonship; his taking human nature into union with his divine nature; his incarnation; his birth; his baptism; his transfiguration; his ministry; his rejection; his death; his resurrection; his ascension; his sending of the Holy Ghost; his ministry from the glory; his coming again.

And more, much more, more of the full range of what he has done for our salvation. And of the revelation by the Son of the Father, of his eternal counsel and purpose in salvation. Moreover of the Person and work of the Holy Ghost, who bringeth salvation into the hearts of his people, thus to unite them together as one in the Lord, an habitation of God through the Spirit. Such fulness of the blessing of the gospel came unto us: 'How then shall they call on him in whom they have not believed? and how shall they believe in him of whom they have not heard? and how shall they hear without a preacher? and how shall they preach except they be sent?'

It was this same gospel of Christ, that which was from the beginning, which came as a balm to our wounded spirits under the preaching which had been sent unto us.

When Mr. Metcalfe had to return to England, however, we were fearful, for we knew not where we could continue to be taught this same word of the truth of the gospel. All our former foundation was sandy. Nothing we had heard before would ever stand the weight of eternity. Looking back now, I realize how much conflict the servant of God must have felt in having to leave us.

This selfsame conflict is that of which the apostle Paul wrote in Colossians and Philippians. For how grave is the responsibility of the ministers of Christ for the souls of God's people, that they would not be beguiled, ensnared, misled, or fall away. And how great the love of the apostles in the beginning. This same fervent love and care were manifestly shown after Mr. Metcalfe's departure in the correspondence between him and those amongst us who wrote to him. Many of us could testify of how much we were comforted, nourished, strengthened, by these epistles of love. To this day, the words of these pastoral letters are etched in our hearts and in our minds.

True to his word, Mr. Metcalfe returned to the Far East. He came again at the commandment of our gracious Father, to labour among us, that we might be built up in our most holy faith. In our sojourn through this great howling wilderness of our pilgrimage, as young babes in Christ, often foolish as sheep that would go astray, often bewildered and ensnared, we were lovingly and carefully shepherded from the left and from the right into the pathway of righteousness.

The precious doctrine of Christ was taught line upon line, precept upon precept to us, and, as a nurse cherisheth her children, so did the true minister of God watch over us in all our affairs, that we might stand perfect and complete in all the will of God.

Introduction

When I read and re-read the letters written to me over the years, I was continually encouraged, admonished, instructed, edified by such spiritual flow of words to the growth and profit of my soul. This experience is shared amongst my sisters, and doubtless my brethren too. Having access to some of the sisters' letters, I felt it meet and right to compile them into a book in the hope and prayer that they would be a source of comfort and edification for many of our dearly beloved brethren and sisters who have gone through like spiritual experiences and travail. The ministry of the word and the Spirit are amply evident and I am certain will be witnessed within the hearts of the readers who are the Lord's sheep.

Seeing the shortness of the time, the great falling away of Christendom, the dearth of priceless spiritual counsel, this book I trust will be valued by godly saints sojourning in this earthly pilgrimage, and received with rejoicing to see the gracious dealings of our God with his people.

To our beloved minister of God, Mr. John Metcalfe, our spiritual father who has begotten us again by the word of the truth of the gospel, that we may know the grace of God in truth, we owe our own selves besides, and desire that we may remain steadfast, immovable, always abounding in the work of the LORD, being of the same mind, of the same love, minding the same things, that we may fulfil his joy, and be his crown and glory in that day.

Above all, we render praise and thanks unto our God and Father who has made us meet to be partakers of the inheritance of the saints in light, and unto our Lord and Saviour Jesus Christ who loved us and gave himself for us.

Now unto him that is able to keep us from falling, and to present us faultless before the presence of his glory with exceeding joy, to the only wise God our Saviour, be glory and majesty, dominion and power, both now and ever. Amen.

Sie Siok Hui,
Singapore.

BALAKRISHNAN PUNITHAVATHI

PASTORAL LETTERS TO
Balakrishnan Punithavathi

John Metcalfe Publishing Trust,
Church Road, Tylers Green,
Penn, Buckinghamshire.

Miss Balakrishnan Punithavathi,
Singapore 1953.   8.3.85

John Metcalfe, an elder, and a slave of Jesus Christ, to beloved sister Punitha, my daughter in the faith:
Grace be to thee, mercy, and peace, from God our Father and the Lord Jesus Christ.

I WAS so thankful to receive your letter, and to have knowledge of the reason why I had not heard from you earlier. I understand and can follow all your pathway, and the reason for my not having heard before. Indeed, you have had a difficult and trying path: 'There is a path which no fowl knoweth, and which the vulture's eye hath not seen.' Nevertheless, He knoweth the way that I take, when he hath tried me, I shall come forth as gold.

Now for the time being, perplexity and doubt becloud and darken the way. But, When my spirit was overwhelmed within me, then thou knewest my path. Be

9

assured the promise is unto you, 'I will bring the blind by a way that they knew not; I will lead them in paths that they have not known: I will make darkness light before them, and crooked things straight. These things will I do unto them, and not forsake them.' Yea, He led them forth by a right way, that they might go to a city of habitation.

You know, you were not without the Lord's work hitherto, and he knoweth them that are his. If you feel ignorant of the foundation, none the less, he has built you upon it, and will send you the knowledge of his work in due season, so that you may grow in grace and in the knowledge of our Lord Jesus Christ.

Do not doubt what the Lord wrought in you before I came, or what you had learned of Christ, or that God himself had favoured you with such a spirit as responded wholly to his truth. Do not allow your feeling of previous ignorance to cause you to doubt what God had wrought in you heretofore, to give you such a sweet and willing spirit of obedience to the truth so far as you knew it, and immediately you saw more of it. Nay, the rather, praise God that he has gone on so wonderfully with such weak, infirm, unstable creatures as we are! Let Christ be all in all, that in all things he may have the pre-eminence.

Now I hope you will receive my letter in a spirit of meekness, and of confidence and trust, and understand that, for the work's sake, I seek to keep those together who have come out, that we may all come together in one in due season, for the truth's sake which dwelleth in us, and shall be with us for ever. Amen.

Now may the Lord Jesus appear in your midst, the doors being locked, and say, Peace be unto you. Yea, may he breathe upon you and say, Peace be unto you. Blessed are the peacemakers, for they shall be called the children of God. But they shall not be called fools, who pour out every word imprudently. No, but their eye is steady upon him who made peace, who is our peace, and who preaches peace, even our Lord and Saviour Jesus Christ.

May I give no offence to my beloved daughter, and our dear sisters, in the things I write from my heart for their good, and the good of Jerusalem. If in anything I appear to confuse them, or there is anything that offends, I beg them to walk in the light and speak to me, as unto a trusted father in Christ, in perfect confidence.

My beloved daughter, there are many questions in your letter, but, believe me, what I have written is the one thing needful. 'And the rest will I set in order when I come.' Pray for me.

My love to my dear daughter,
The grace of our Lord Jesus Christ be with you all.

John Metcalfe

II John 12.

John Metcalfe Publishing Trust,
Church Road, Tylers Green,
Penn, Buckinghamshire.

Miss Balakrishnan Punithavathi,
Singapore 1953.   1.5.85

John Metcalfe, a servant of God and of the Lord Jesus
Christ, to my well-beloved daughter Punitha, whom I
love in the truth:
Grace be unto thee, mercy, and peace, from God our
Father and the Lord Jesus Christ.

I GIVE thanks without ceasing that God himself has
written with his finger upon the fleshy table of your
heart, making you to know wisdom in the hidden parts,
and truth in the inward man. And what wisdom is this?
Why, that of God in Christ Jesus made unto thee wisdom,
both righteousness, sanctification, and redemption. In
him are hid all the treasures of wisdom and knowledge,
and, ye are complete in him.

What wisdom, to see Christ crucified with the eye of
faith, to draw in the atonement to the breast with the
hand of faith, and, believing with the heart, to enfold a
crucified Redeemer in all the delights of love and devotion:
'We love him, because he first loved us.'

What wisdom, to see our sanctification in Another,
obtained fully by his sacrifice, 'For by one offering he
hath perfected for ever them that are sanctified', and, if
so, presented by him on our behalf before the throne of
grace. Then, to embrace with joy and thanksgiving One

12

who has already made us holy and without blame before the Father in love; yea, and more yet, as the fountain of life springs up in the believing heart, and the well-spring of gratitude breaks forth, the Holy Ghost being given, to feel and know the work of faith whereby we cry Abba, Father.

Then spiritual and experimental sanctification, separation to God and the Father, become really outworked from the inner man to every member of the body, and throughout the pathway in which we walk, that we might be a sweet savour of Christ to Godward.

What wisdom, to hope in a Redeemer that shall change this vile body, that it might be like unto his glorious body! What wisdom, I say, to be wise virgins with oil in our vessels with our lamps; to heed the midnight cry; to go out to meet the Bridegroom; to go into the very wedding feast: wisdom indeed, unknown to fools who trust in themselves, not making Jesus Christ their all in all.

What wisdom, to await the return of the Lord, 'to wait for his Son from heaven', to be ready for the shout, the archangel's voice, and the trump of God; to walk soberly, godly, and righteously, withal filled with joy in believing, and hope in praying, and love in the Father and the Son, whilst beholding the King in his beauty, in the land that is very far off: Oh, my daughter, see that thus thou hast 'an inheritance among them which are sanctified by faith that is in me.'

Yet, be it so, we must bear the yoke in our youth. None teacheth like him, and, every man that hath heard, and hath learned of the Father, cometh unto him. Moreover, the law proves a schoolmaster to bring us to Christ. 'Blessed is the man whom thou chastenest, O LORD, and teachest out of thy law.' This teaching brings in cutting convictions, sharp rebukes, and all the thunders of Sinai; blackness comes down on the soul, rebellion rises, daring thoughts against God fill the mind, corruptions flood the heart: the soul cries, My wounds stink by reason of my corruption.

With horror one views the filth and depravity, the arrogance and unbelief within, and straightway despair overcomes the spirit. Now dryness and barrenness, chains and bondage, guilt and remorse, claim full possession, and bring the fainting soul to the brink of despair: 'I had fainted, unless I had believed to see the goodness of the LORD in the land of the living.'

And yet, all this law-work is but the teaching of the Father, to bring the soul off self-righteousness, off carnal ease, off presumptuous religion, false-faith, and human sentiment; so that, convicted, nigh unto death, full of groaning and misery, the soul is taught the lesson, the grand lesson, by the Teacher of teachers, by the Light himself, CHRIST IS OUR ALL, HIS ATONEMENT RENDERED FULL SATISFACTION, AND HIS GRACE IS SUFFICIENT FOR EVERY NEED.

Now, the altogether lovely Redeemer appears again to the chastened child: faith revives, the sweetness of pardoning love sets the eye to weeping with joy and contrition together, and the sacrifice of Christ appears with such an abundance of grace, mercy, and peace to the soul, that one sinks to the feet of the Saviour, rejoicing with joy unspeakable and full of glory.

Now, this is the way of the just. Here are the footsteps of the flock. And in this way shall my daughter possess the rest that remaineth to the people of God. Not by what she does, but by what HE has done, is doing, and shall accomplish. Not by working, but by believing. Not by the law, but by grace. Thus is brought in the true repentance, not to be repented of, and the true holiness, which shall ever please the Father of lights, with whom is no variableness, neither shadow of turning.

And this shall be the portion of my beloved Punitha, world without end. Amen.

So saith a slave of Jesus Christ,

John Metcalfe

Share this letter with Lai Yok and Kam Yen, and let them know how moved I am at the love and concern shown to me by all. Truly, I am filled with joy, and my cup runneth over, being touched beyond measure that you should show such love.

The grace of our Lord Jesus Christ
be with your spirit. Amen.

Temple Orchard,
High Wycombe,
Buckinghamshire.

Miss Balakrishnan Punithavathi,
Bethany Meeting Hall,
Singapore 1129.   14.9.87

My very dear sister in Christ,

GRACE be unto you, mercy, and peace, from God our
Father and the Lord Jesus Christ. Your excellent
and informative letter brought rejoicing to my heart, to
know that Christ is your all-in-all, the joy and praise of
your heart, the peace of your conscience, the light of your
life, the life of your spirit, the guide of your understanding, and the love of your being. Christ is all. Of God we
are in him, who of God is made unto us wisdom. We
know our darkness, yes, but we know his light. We know
our ignorance, true, but we know his wisdom.

And what wisdom is this, that is a Person, Christ himself? It is the wisdom of God. And to whom is this Person
the wisdom of God? To the poor, base, ignorant, to the
vile, empty, and dark. It is of God that such lost creatures
are found in Christ Jesus, just as it is of him that Christ
has become their wisdom. 'But of him are ye in Christ
Jesus, who of God is made unto us wisdom', I Cor. 1:30.

And what is our wisdom, that stands in Christ? That
we are made wise to know the filth and corruption of our
natures, and the sinfulness of even our religious works.
Then, that we hate and abhor our own righteousness. If
so, that our righteousness is in him, and stands by faith

in his blood. He is our justification. Rejoice in this, yea, rejoice with exceeding joy: Christ is our justification.

He is our sanctification. Sanctification is not something to which we are to attain. It is something which we have in Christ, it is our wisdom to rest in it, and be glad. Here is our ministry, here is our church, here is our certain dwelling! How faith delights to credit all the glory of Christ, to own all that he has done, and all that he is, exulting in the same. This is our possession and inheritance. Faith receives of his fulness, and grace for grace.

And our redemption. The glory is before us. 'We have redemption through his blood.' God has made Christ unto us redemption. It is not a thing for which we must cry, sigh, pant, or long: we have it. God has made him redemption to us: he has done it. Then, rejoice in the Lord, and again I say, Rejoice.

I continue to suffer continual insults and foul abuse, which is heaped upon me from all quarters daily. It is good to be humbled, to be kept still, to be restrained from retaliation, to be reserved from wrath. Praise the Lord, all these things are turned to good, and, indeed, how vile and corrupt, how foul and unfit, I am! Let them heap iniquity upon me, let them raise the strife of tongues, let them persecute, let them vilify and slander me: 'Let them curse, but bless thou', Psalm 109:28. In all this, I but follow the path of the just, and, besides, it provides an affliction that purifies as does a furnace.

I am not delivered from the worst, longest, and most damaging trial of all. I do not want to go into details, but I beg and entreat the prayers of my dear sister and daughter in the Lord, that God may grant me a great deliverance, and set me free from the damage caused— and that could still be caused—by the adversaries. Do, I beseech, pray for me until these calamities be overpast.

The Meeting here goes on well, I humbly thank and praise God, and brethren grow in grace, and in the knowledge of our Lord and Saviour Jesus Christ.

I know that it is hard for you, but I believe that with faith the Lord will lead you out into a wealthy place wherein you shall praise him. The present afflictions are but for a moment, they are the valley of Baca, but you who weep therein are not alone, the rain also filleth the pools, and every one of the faithful weepers shall appear before God in Zion, and cry, 'Alleluia: for the Lord God omnipotent reigneth'. Say unto Zion, Thy God reigneth!

My fervent love to all the saints.

The grace of our Lord Jesus Christ be with thy spirit.

John Metcalfe

Balakrishnan Punithavathi

John Metcalfe Publishing Trust,
Church Road, Tylers Green,
Penn, Buckinghamshire.

Miss Balakrishnan Punithavathi,
Singapore 1953.   2.2.88

My dearly beloved and favoured daughter, whom I love
in the truth, and not I only, but also all they that have
known the truth:
Grace be with you, mercy, and peace, from God the
Father, and from the Lord Jesus Christ, the Son of the
Father, in truth and love.

YOUR letter brought such a fragrance of Christ, and
so much of the earnest of the Holy Ghost, that I
could not but praise our God and Father, who hath
chosen us in Christ, and given us the promise of eternal
life before the world was, that he should have shown such
love and favour unto my dear daughter.

And now through him who hath loved us, and washed
us from our sins in his own blood, and made us kings
and priests unto our God, may this same earnest spirit,
and panting zeal, be with you all the days of your life,
and may he preserve, keep, and bless you abundantly,
to his own everlasting praise and glory. Amen.

Now let me tell you immediately that I intend in the will
of God to be in Penang from the 11th to the 20th of the
third month inclusive, in some few weeks time. If it is
possible for any of you to come for that time, or part of
that time, or even on the seventh and first day, my joy
would be fulfilled.

19

You know that I feel for you all the inexpressible love of God in Christ, as I believe you do for me. May God and our Father enable us to receive from his own dear Son, by the Holy Ghost from heaven, at this time of refreshing. May his providence open the way at least in part, and at least for some. Whether it be so or not, if the Lord will, I shall surely be there.

I will not at this time write much. Only I entreat you, my dear Punitha, to tell Kala I am deeply touched before the Lord at her kind message and love, and in the savour of the love of Christ, and of God and our Father, I would convey my love in the Spirit to her. Tell her that early every morning her name is on my lips before the throne of grace, and that in the very presence of him before whom the seraphim hide their faces, crying, Holy, holy, holy, Lord God Almighty, by the blood of Jesus Christ, and through faith in his name, I make intercession and supplication on her behalf. The Lord comfort her, and console her in the knowledge that her trials and afflictions are ordered for her good, and, persevering through them, will bring great good and blessing.

Now, Puni, heed my words. If the Lord gives you to receive it, her wise word to you was most true. It is her experience. Nevertheless, all must be in the gift of God. I believe that the Lord has reserved you for himself, and that he has a purpose for you, and will make great use of you. But it will not be soon. Many years of refining, suffering, winnowing, and chastisement must pass. But in the end, when spiritual maturity has been reached, much nearer my age than yours, you will bear much fruit, walking in the way, taking up your cross daily, and following him. Heed Kala's admonition, if God so grant to you in liberty. And, if you walk circumspectly, if it be in liberty, and the gift of God, you will find these words to come true.

My dear daughter, whose discretion, carefulness, and holy zeal I so much respect, withal your unselfish and devout love for Christ and his people: the Lord bless you and keep you.

With my unfeigned and fervent love in the truth,
Your father in Christ,

John Metcalfe

Temple Orchard,
High Wycombe,
Buckinghamshire.

Miss Balakrishnan Punithavathi,
Singapore 1953.   29.9.88

My dearly beloved daughter in Christ,

GRACE be unto thee, mercy, and peace, from God our Father and the Lord Jesus Christ.

The letters which you sent were a great encouragement to me, and I give thanks at every remembrance of my dear daughter.

Over the past months I knew in my spirit that you were in trials and temptations. However James exhorts you to 'count it all joy when ye fall into divers temptations.' And, again, 'Blessed is the man that endureth temptation: for when he is tried, he shall receive the crown of life, which the Lord hath promised to them that love him.'

This, Peter confirms, saying, 'Beloved, think it not strange concerning the fiery trial which is'—mark that, which is—'to try you, as though some strange thing happened unto you: but rejoice, inasmuch as ye are partakers of Christ's sufferings; that, when his glory shall be revealed, ye may be glad also with exceeding joy.'

But why should these trials seem strange? Why should we be shaken by temptations when we are tried? Why is it a 'fiery' trial? Why, because of what comes to light, which fills us with horror, and brings us down to the depths, so that we might despair even of life itself.

It is like Paul's experience under the law: 'I was alive without the law'—that is, without it being applied to the inward man convincingly: when it was just opinion and sentiment—'but when the commandment came'—that is, inwardly by the Holy Ghost, convicting of the strictness of the commandment, the rigour of the law, the holiness of God, and the hidden enmity of the flesh—'sin revived, and I died.'

Balakrishnan Punithavathi

In a sense, this is just what happens to us under gospel trials. I knew that soon this must happen to you, and I knew in my spirit when it happened to you. Don't think it strange: it is a mark of sonship, a proof of election.

Yet it seems otherwise, for corruption is discovered, enmity is brought to light, inability, deadness, darkness, groaning follow, and bands and chains hold us fast under a rising tide of offensive and hateful carnality. Then despair is at our right hand, we feel we are too foul to be the Lord's, too filthy to pray, and we sink down in misery and self-pity, as a sour, grudging spirit takes us, with resentment against our lot working away at the heart.

Thus the fire has brought to light the dross and scum, while under the burning heat of cross providences and sharp temptations filth rises to the surface, till we can see nothing else. Before, we seemed to be going on well, we felt our ardent zeal, our burning love for the Lord, and, if we felt corruptions at all, they were eclipsed by the radiance of his countenance. Alas! No more. Now all we see is our rottenness, all we feel is our corruption, our flesh seethes, we stink in our own nostrils.

This is his work: it is all his discovering our state to ourselves, that his grace might be magnified. So ready are we to think some good of ourselves, to suppose we are superior in religion, all very spiritual, that we have done so well: yet we are all filth and corruption, and nothing but grace, free grace, through faith, can save us. And it does save us. 'By grace are ye saved through faith; and that not of yourselves: it is the gift of God: not of works, lest any man should boast.'

Yet boast we will, even in heart, whilst feigning humility. But when the fiery trial comes, when temptations compass us about, when afflictions bind us fast, then our true state is discovered to us, and we realize what we can never learn any other way.

First, we realize that in us, that is, in our flesh, there dwelleth no good thing; and there never will. And second, we realize that grace, grace, grace, the grace of God in Christ, saved us, and will save us, and that this is all from the love of God, outside of ourselves, and all despite ourselves. Now, these are the inward lessons God is teaching you, my dearly beloved Puni.

What a favour! To be taught of God? You, or me? Such filthy, worthless, useless creatures. Nevertheless, it is so, that his grace might be magnified in the meanest vessels, that all the praise might be to him. Yes, he is teaching you, and this is your glory; praise him in the fires, rejoice with joy unspeakable and full of glory in your trials, for no bastard ever knew this chastening, and no bondchild ever received such scourging.

Oh, what kindness! Do count it all joy. It is wonderful of him to do this for you, wonderful. Wonderful, that you might really see just how unworthy you are of the unutterable love which he has bestowed upon you in Christ.

Yes, go to Penang. I hope to be there well before the meetings, and will then meet with any who come earlier.

24

But let all attend the days of meetings themselves, whilst any that can or may wish to, are welcome to come before.

My earnest and spiritual love to you, my dear,

Yours in grace,

John Metcalfe

LEE LYE SIM

THE TESTIMONY OF
Lee Lye Sim

Singapore

10.6.90

I WAS a fool that said in my heart 'There is no God', for I had lived out the early years of my life in ungodliness. My childhood days were spent in much ease and pleasure. I had no religion.

The times which I had anything to do with something near religion were when my grandmother desired me to help her in preparing the joss papers. At a certain time of the year, she remembers the death of her ancestors. Much food would be prepared and laid on a table with lighted candles on the forefront of the table. She would pull me along with her to kneel and bow before the table of food and candles with joss sticks in my hand. The joss papers were burnt later. Each time when I was made to do it, an uncomfortable feeling was in me. I suppose it was more of pride that I felt ridiculous, being found in such a posture.

I remember an incident at school. The senior teacher raised a question at a school assembly. She asked for a show of hands of those who believed the existence of God. A number of hands were raised but I laughed and scorned at them and said to myself—there is no God. I was twelve years old then.

That which occupied me at the time was satisfying my greedy appetite for food, having fun, and school. Not that I was studious. I had favours from teachers because of my brother. In that way, I was to maintain a reputation as a good student for the honour of my parents. I was a self-righteous hypocrite in school. My head was filled with pride—thinking myself to be something. The mischiefs I did in secret were hid from teachers. I was a liar and a tale-bearer. I was disobedient to my parents with rebellion in the heart when punished. I hated work and I was delighted at every opportunity to escape any house chores.

The fear of hell took hold of me when I was thirteen. My brother met a young man at the Stadium in a sports meet, who told him of sin, death, hell, and of Jesus Christ the Saviour. When my brother came home, he related all that he heard to us. I was convinced of hell. My brother was very sober and serious when he spoke those words, which was unlike him. I went away and in secret prayed the 'sinner's prayer' which was to confess one's sins, to ask for forgiveness for one's sins, to open one's heart, and to accept Jesus into the heart as Saviour. But there was no peace in my heart. Whenever I felt that fear, I repeated the 'sinner's prayer'. I tried to cast away my fears by occupying myself with something to do but was not successful.

After some time, I could not contain it any more. I spoke to my brother and told him my trouble. He enquired whether I had prayed the 'sinner's prayer'. I replied I had done so and many times over. He suggested attending the meetings—'worship service' and Sunday school at 'JSM', where he had already been. He also instructed me to read the bible daily. So I kept up bible reading, as conscientiously as I could, for I felt if I failed to, I would have sinned. But I could not understand what I read and soon it became a weariness.

It was much later that I attended the service and Sunday school, being hindered by my mother—not that she was against the Christian religion but more so for my safety. Before that, I had almost involved myself in becoming a member of the 'Youth For Christ' group, after having met a few members in one of their meetings. This went on without my mother's knowledge during school hours. Two of my classmates were with that group and persuaded me to join them, which I did. My brother discovered the matter and warned me to leave, to which I submitted.

It was after much persuasion and assurance from my brother, that my mother allowed me to go to the meetings at the Mission. I did not attend the 'worship service' in the morning regularly. I had difficulty understanding the message the 'reverend' or a brother gave. Besides I felt quite lost when I was there. I was separated from my brother. He had to sit on a different row of benches from me as the men and women had to be seated on different rows. Sunday school was better to me for at least I could receive some knowledge and understanding of the bible.

I was still troubled about my salvation. Someone from the Mission showed and explained to me from I John chapter 5, verse 13, that it is a matter of believing and knowing and not according to feelings, when I told her my feelings and questions on the salvation of my soul. Hence, this became my answer each time my doubts arose.

Later, to my disappointment, I learnt that there were 'dos' and 'don'ts' which were expected of us to keep. Two of which I found great difficulty giving them up. That was the television and cinema. In the afternoon, after Sunday school, I was back home, in front of the television. There were times my brother invited people from the Mission to the house. Whenever I knew they were coming, or heard their voices from outside the house, how I hurried to shut the television and hid myself in the room. I felt rotten and guilty of such hypocrisy. I was a television addict and to me it was impossible to leave it off.

I was baptized by a 'reverend' the next year. Soon afterwards, I grew weary. Much of my time and energy were spent on my school work and activities. Little time was given to reading the bible and my attendance of the meetings was irregular. And as a major examination drew near, and for want of time to prepare for it, I had stopped going to the meetings. Having passed the examination, I went for a further stage of study at a college. Over there, I met two members of the Mission, who persuaded me to join them in their bible study in another member's house, which I did but I went not to the meetings. They asked me the reason for not being present on Sunday meetings. I made excuses.

After I left college, I took a job in an accounting firm. During the first year in that company, I was miserable. I made a profession of the Christian religion before my work colleagues. The things taught from 'JSM' still remained in me but I compromised. I would not go to the cinema for a show, but the television was alright. As for music; country and sentimental music were alright but no, not the pop or rock music. I kept worldly, short hair style, was taken away with worldly chit-chat and jokes and kept worldly companionship. The love of the world was in my heart. In fact I broke many of the 'JSM' rules.

But conscience was troubled. I could not give clear answers to some of the questions put forth by my colleagues. I was deeply miserable. Although I did enjoy the pleasures of this life for a season, it was for a season only. I soon found life totally meaningless and deep within I felt that great emptiness. I wished to die then but thought to myself, any suicidal move would stumble my colleagues. Now, nothing could satisfy me—not any worldly entertainment. I was nineteen then.

I went back to religion and desired to take it seriously. I kept consistent reading of the bible. The lack of courage and pride kept me back from going to the Mission. For shame, that people should see me in this backslidden state. My younger sister, whom I had observed had become serious and fervent in the Christian religion, had been to the Mission regularly for some months. One night, she approached me and spoke to me: encouraged me to come back. I decided to humble myself and went. Some at the Mission recognized me and were glad for me. I was encouraged.

It happened, at that time, the Mission property was to be taken away by the authorities, and we had not many months to hold our meetings in the premises. My sister and I went to as many meetings as we possibly could. I thought I was revived. I read the bible more carefully and found myself able to pray in the meetings. I went house to house tracting and desired much to be at the meetings.

In 1984 I thought I was called into full-time service. When I read the scriptures, passages, I thought then, seemed to speak to me, to call me aside to serve the Lord, and messages which I heard from the meetings seemed to confirm it. I sought counsel. I was encouraged into it by one of the 'pastors' of the Mission, besides the leader of my group, and also by a missioner. My heart was set on doing it; to leave my job and join the Mission. But I was fearful of the consequences to be faced with my parents. When I broke the news to my mother, she was shocked and surprised. My father objected to the whole idea and was very grieved when I actually did it.

I was guided by a missioner for a time, I had much time on my hands. Honestly, I was quite lost. I did not know what to do. My quiet time stretched longer in the morning. I spent most of the day reading the scriptures but did find, most of the time, that my reading was dry. My prayers were with much crying often, feeling the absence of God's presence. I had wanted to serve the Lord and please him but found his face hid from me. A voice sounded in my heart—what of your past sins! I felt his wrath gone forth against me in that the heavens were as brass. I cried to him for mercy but felt that he would not hear me because of all my iniquities. I wished I could go back in time to put things right.

Sometimes, I sat in my room for an hour or more staring blankly onto the wall and the ceiling, in much despair. But I hid my condition from the missioner, the 'pastor', and members in the Mission. I kept up tracting, visiting, and accompanying the missioner to places and bible studies at times. I kept myself occupied with reading books on prayer, devotion, revivals, and so on. I felt tried, and thought maybe I should go to a bible college to be taught and trained to become a missioner. I think I would have if I had been sent.

I was quite disappointed when I did not receive any monetary support from the Mission as most of the full-timers and missioners had. I had given all that I had to the Mission. I felt very bitter, and murmurings were in my heart when I was, at times, left with no money for food or transport expenses. Then afterwards, I would condemn myself for feeling thus and for such thoughts. So I gave tuition to earn my keep.

A trip to Kuala Lumpur and Ipoh was organized in the year 1984 and I was to go to evangelize to the Malays because I knew their language. So I went and stayed in Kuala Lumpur at the Mission premises for a month. I was in much fear, feeling my incapability to help in any way to the work in Kuala Lumpur. And I was still troubled with the guilt of my sins unpardoned. Each time, to feel that I may pray aright to God, I made a confession of my sins. But there were times I felt my sins to be so dark, so grievous in the sight of God, that they could not be pardoned.

I remember, in one overnight prayer meeting, in Kuala Lumpur, in the midst of my earnest crying and weeping because of my sins, these words came to me: Daughter, be of good cheer, thy sins be forgiven thee. I ceased from my crying, and lifted myself up from the posture of prayer. I think I never felt such a peace in my heart and my heart was filled with joy. I could not rest that night; pondering and wondering at those words.

In that same year, in the twelfth month 1984, in Penang, there was to be a conference. And I learnt that a guest speaker from England was to address us in the evening meetings. I did not think much about it but, on the contrary, was wary of him because of some negative remarks the 'pastor', the missioner, and some others had made on him. But when I first heard him speak, and at the end of his first address, I said within my heart—never man spake like this man. I longed to hear him speak and looked forward to every evening.

I pondered much about this man, Mr. John Metcalfe, and the things which he spoke. In fact, I did not, at first, even know how his name was spelt. To me, he was a great speaker, and a very spiritual pastor of a church in England, and there should be, as I felt, that distance to be kept. But I found that he was also kind, gentle, and considerate. He spoke to us freely and gave help when counsel was sought from him. I tried to grasp and retain every word he spoke.

In his first address, from I Thessalonians chapter 1, one question he asked before all of us remained in my heart. That was, Do we answer to the church as it is in God the Father and in the Lord Jesus Christ? I could not answer that question positively for I felt that in the light of that which Mr. Metcalfe brought forth of her characteristics, we did not measure to it. I doubted my salvation also. I was much encouraged from the words in his address from Psalm 11. They brought hope in his word.

I was delighted to know that later he would come to Singapore to address us. Though I could not fully understand or grasp all that the servant of the Lord spoke, at that time, there were other simple and plain issues which remained and troubled my heart and conscience. Issues such as the headship of Christ, and the distinction to be observed between men and women in the church.

I became aware of the apostolic ordinance of the covering of the head of the woman when she prays or prophesies, which we did not observe or keep; of the apostle not suffering women to speak in the church, which we did, both in our Missions, and in the full-time service. I went back home and pondered upon the words. But I did not want to pursue further into the matters, so I cast aside all questions.

However, I did not have any rest, and in Mr. Metcalfe's last address in Singapore from Psalm 133, the words came with power and I was convicted in my heart. The words were so plain and clear, speaking to our states and conditions, one could not make them out to be of other meaning, nor find excuses.

But to my grief, the leaders of the Mission, and many who had heard these words, refused to obey the word of God, which they claimed they loved, boasting of being such fundamentalists in practice. Instead, they spoke evil of Mr. Metcalfe after he returned to England. A number of us left the Mission, seeing the impossibility to continue except the whole system be discarded and begin again with obedience to the word of God.

As I recall these things that have happened, I am thankful to the Lord for his mercy and the deliverance granted from the net of this legal system and its entangling errors. Though I had thought that I would stay in the Mission and serve therein for the rest of my life and had always thought their teachings to be right, yet to turn from this system of works and to take the step of obeying God's word by faith alone, I know it to be possible only by his grace and strength. And at that point of time, I felt as if all that I had trusted in and built upon was being crushed and destroyed and that there was no standing ground any more.

Mr. Metcalfe had to return to England for the unfinished work of writing 'The Hymns of the New Testament', and we hoped that he would be back shortly in the same year. Meantime, a former 'pastor' from the Mission led us in the group. After a while, I found a job.

During that time, I was under deep conviction of my sins and sinful state. My past sins were brought to my remembrance again and I was tormented in my mind, that they had not been forgiven. I asked, What shall I do? I also found myself sinning and continually sinning, in every hour that I was awake. I found myself sinning with my heart, with my mind, with my mouth, and with my deeds. I was unable to put forth a good or a right thought.

All manner of uncleanness and filthiness rose in my thoughts. It was with much regret that I ever did fill my

mind with the filth and corruption from the television
and worldly books, for these things came back to my
mind and I found no strength not to remember or think
of them. Besides, my heart did delight in them. I groaned
over the state of my heart; wishing that I could really
have a heart transplant. 'For out of the heart proceed
evil thoughts, murders, adulteries, fornications, thefts,
false witness, blasphemies.'

I discovered my heart to be deceitful above all things
and desperately wicked. And worse, I had whitewashed
my true state with religion. I had made clean the outside
by going to church, reading the bible, praying, doing
'good' to others, helping the poor, and abstaining from
worldly entertainment but, inside, the heart was unclean,
insincere, untrue, impure, worldly, ungodly, which appeared not to man.

Every motive, every desire, and every deed done were
from self-interest. The desire for man to think one to be
saintly, religious, good, and among Christians, as someone spiritual and zealous. Each time, when I would sneer
or think ill of a drug addict, or a murderer, or a thief, or
an harlot, my heart would be smitten as I remembered
the words of the Pharisee: God, I thank thee that I am
not as other men are. But I was as other men are, if not
worse, because of my hypocrisy and dishonesty.

I heard as if the Lord did say to me; I know you, that
you have not the love of God in you. I opened not my
mouth as far as possible, for I would condemn myself for
the words that came forth. The more I sought to do good,
the more evil was present with me. It was as if God had
placed a large mirror before me, only this time it was for

the inward man. And I saw my true state and was horrified by it. I was in a bitter and peevish spirit. I cursed the day I was born and wished that I had never been born. I desired to end my life and would have, were it not, I believe now, for the mercies of the Lord that prevented me. For at each try, the fear of death and the judgment ahead seized me.

My eyes were sore from weeping, I would go to bed as early as I could and make myself sleep, for then I would not be conscious for a while. Each day was a dread. I spoke to no one except for a sister, who had helped me and encouraged me to wait and hope. My work colleagues looked upon me with strangeness. I hardly spoke a word to them except about work. I had not gone to the meetings held by the former missioner, except on the first days and certain evenings when I was virtually forced to go. For I found this man brought more darkness and confusion upon my mind. He knew not nor could understand my state. He blamed a few others for their influence over me, hence bringing me into such a 'morbid' state as they called it.

One of them, a former missioner from 'JSM', came to visit me and counselled me to walk according to the word of God and not experiences or feelings. But I found the Psalms, the language of the psalmist, spoke to my heart. Though I may not have gone through the depth of the experience the psalmist had, that he should pray or cry thus, yet I could agree with the psalmist. I knew, in some measure, what he was talking about. And I found reading the Psalms such a delight and comfort to my soul. I read and re-read time and again the Psalms like Psalm 42, 38, 88, 142, and 143.

Mr. Metcalfe's letter on the 19th of the fourth month, 1985, in reply to my letter to him, brought me to hope and to wait upon the Lord. I was astonished at the contents of the letter. For I knew not that what was happening to me was the work of God. In my unbelief I said, How could this disgusting and contemptible creature be a child of God?

I was overjoyed when Mr. Metcalfe came back to Singapore in the seventh month, 1985. And in his first address from Titus chapter 2, verse 11, my unbelief and hardness of heart were broken. As the truth of God's salvation was opened up, I was glad to behold the salvation which God the Father had purposed, outwrought by his Son, without us having the need to do anything, and not only so but that the Holy Ghost should come to bring this salvation into our hearts. And I believed.

The grace of God that bringeth salvation had appeared unto me. His love, the love of God, my Saviour, for me, overwhelmed my heart. My eyes were a fountain of tears, weeping for joy and relief. Truly it was renewal to my soul. He heals the broken-hearted and binds their wounds. I rejoiced with joy unspeakable and full of glory. There was a deep peace in my heart and my soul was brought into rest. His longsuffering is salvation. He hears the groanings of the prisoners and the sighs of the poor and needy.

I am thankful that God did send his servant, Mr. Metcalfe, into our midst at Penang and Singapore, that the true gospel of our Lord Jesus Christ should be preached unto us. And also that we have been taught the precious doctrine of Christ and been brought under this ministry,

which is not a ministry of condemnation but of free justification by grace, of life, and of the Spirit.

Blessed be God, which hath not turned away my prayer,
nor his mercy from me.

Lee Lye Sim

PASTORAL LETTERS TO
Lee Lye Sim

John Metcalfe Publishing Trust,
Church Road, Tylers Green,
Penn, Buckinghamshire.

Miss Lee Lye Sim,
Singapore 1336.   19.4.85

John Metcalfe, a servant of God and of the Lord Jesus Christ, to Lee Lye Sim, in the valley of Baca, beneath clouds of darkness, beset by self-doubts, tormented by the cruel darts of the adversary, afflicted by temptations within and without, and full of fainting and weakness: Grace, mercy, and peace, from God our Father and the Lord Jesus Christ.

BUT you are not alone. No, not even within your heart are you alone. For saith the holy man, He knoweth the way that I take, when he hath tried me, I shall come forth as gold. Then, though nothing but trial was felt, and nothing but trials appeared to the soul, so that one might say, 'Are his mercies gone for ever?', yet, it is HE that trieth me. When the trials pass, the Tryer will appear for who he is: the great God and our Saviour Jesus Christ.

Now, thou art in heaviness through manifold temptations; this is the fiery trial, the trial of your faith.

In the fire, what can you expect? Pain. Sorrow. Burning. The rising up of scum, dross, filth. No feeling or sense of the Lord, only of the furnace. Nevertheless, He shall sit as a refiner and purifier of the sons of Levi. He sits outside the furnace: they are refined in it. But he is in control. When he hath tried me, I shall come forth as gold. If you say, But all I see is filth and dross; I reply, This is sure proof that you are being refined of the Lord. What other than the furnace brings the base scum out of the heart of the metal, to leave the pure gold refined? And what gold put itself in the furnace? It is he himself who governs this matter.

This you must believe. The words of the Lord are pure words, as silver tried in a furnace of earth seven times. Your experience is common to God's people, and to none other. Rejoice therefore! What can a man see? Were not three men bound and cast into the midst of the fire? But, lo, 'I see four men loose, walking in the midst of the fire, and they have no hurt; and the form of the fourth is like the Son of God.'

For now you can hardly feel this. You feel alone. But, I will never leave thee, nor forsake thee. I will send you another Comforter. However, the fire, the chastening, you must endure, and endure you shall. This shall, and must, bring to the surface all the dross of self-doubt, all the filth of the flesh, suffered by all the redeemed since the foundation of the world. 'I know that in me (that is, in my flesh,) dwelleth no good thing.' But what godless man ever knew that? But you know it, Lye Sim. Then, you are Paul's companion, and my daughter.

Yes, of course I understand your questions. But I understand more than your questions, and see more than you write. Did you not know this of me, Lye Sim? And do you not know that you can trust me? Pour out your heart to him, at the throne of grace, in the place where blood is sprinkled. When I see the blood, I will pass over you. We have the remission of sins through his blood.

And, believe me, he presides over your afflictions, because he is the Captain of your salvation. If you wish to tell me more, be assured of my total confidence, and my willingness to carry your case to the throne of grace, because I believe wholly in his love for you, my dear. Grace be with thee.

Pray for an effectual door to be opened unto me for his name's sake. Rejoice, and sing psalms. Be whole-hearted in praise, and reading the scriptures, whatever you feel. Depart from evil, and do good.

And the God of peace shall be with you.

The rest shall await my coming, or your further letter.

With love from a slave of Jesus Christ,

John Metcalfe

John Metcalfe Publishing Trust,
Church Road, Tylers Green,
Penn, Buckinghamshire.

Miss Lee Lye Sim,
Singapore 1336.   20.6.85

John Metcalfe, a servant of God and of the Lord Jesus
Christ, to Lee Lye Sim, my daughter in the faith:
Grace, mercy, and peace, from God our Father and the
Lord Jesus Christ.

I GIVE thanks to God that, notwithstanding all the
difficulty and hardness of the way, you are continuing
faithfully and are found obedient to the gospel even to
this day. I know that it is a time of dryness and of famine
with you. That you wander in the wilderness and feel that
you have lost your way.

Be it so, the Shepherd of Israel finds lost sheep, and
none other. He comforts the afflicted, loves the poor,
relieves the distressed, and hearkens to the cry of the
humble. All these states the very circumstances you find
so trying, and are tempted to escape, have produced in
your soul. But because they are hard to bear, and puzzling
to understand, they make you doubt.

Doubt no more. God has ordained this way, and all
these circumstances, for your chastening and profit. And
though you do not now feel it, these very things show his
love for you. Whom the Lord loveth he chasteneth.
Others, he leaves to their false joy and rotten religion. If

46

the circumstances he has chosen to bring this chastening appear strange, What is that to you? Your circumstances are his providences.

Of course this casts you upon the Lord in faith, to believe despite the appearances: but then, so did it for ten thousands before you, as saith the psalmist, Psalm 142:3, When my spirit was overwhelmed within me, then thou knewest my path. It is not that the psalmist knew, his faith was not equal to that, but it was that he knew the Lord had led him into this way, and therefore though he felt lost, he knew that the Lord would lead him through. Hence he says, not that he himself knew, but the LORD knew his path. And there, his faith rested in quietness.

Now, do thou likewise, Lye Sim, and trust him in quiet confidence despite all that is about and within you.

Pray much, and sigh often, and desire constantly my return in the will of the Lord. Amen.

With my love in Christ,

John Metcalfe

Temple Orchard,
High Wycombe,
Buckinghamshire.

Miss Lee Lye Sim,
Singapore 1336.   12.10.87

My very dear daughter in the faith,

G RACE be unto thee, mercy, and peace, from God
our Father and the Lord Jesus Christ.

   With thanksgiving and praise I received your letter, and
rejoiced to know of your steadfastness in the midst of
afflictions within and without. These are the footsteps
of the flock, the marks of the sheep, and sure signs of the
people of God under the immediate dealings of God their
Saviour. The LORD redeemeth the soul of his servants,
and none of them that trust in him shall be desolate,
Ps. 34:22.

   And, if he redeems their souls that are already his
servants, it speaks of our soul, or inward, sense of spiritual
bankruptcy, of our spiritual poverty, of our terrifying
emptiness, and of our having nothing to pay or to provide
for all the crying necessities of our pathway. Then, having
nothing, being barren and destitute, we cry for help. 'The
LORD redeemeth the soul of his servants.'

   And, as to desolation, bear witness, my dear sister, bear
witness, the only desolation you ever knew came before

you really knew him. Afterwards, you were brought, and are brought, to the edge of desolation, but no further. 'None of them that trust in him shall be desolate.'

I know that the Lord has touched and captured your heart, that he has won your affections, and that he has set his love upon you. With these priceless treasures, what is man, the fallen church, the lost world, time, or the present creation? Nothing; less than nothing. Only the present pilgrimage, passing by other people and relation-ships, through different circumstances and changing situations, with altering phases and experiences, these teach us the worthlessness of the flesh, the world, of all that is of man, and the inestimable treasure, the priceless worth of Jesus Christ and his gospel.

'That I may know him' can only be answered in cor-respondence to the knowledge of the world's emptiness, self's bankruptcy, and the law's inability. Then, with that knowledge, the soul cries, 'Hear my prayer, O LORD, and give ear unto my cry; hold not thy peace at my tears: for I am a stranger with thee, and a sojourner, as all my fathers were', Ps. 39:12.

So you see, all your experiences are those of the saints, reflected in a thousand places in the Psalms and elsewhere, and can never be the experience of any other.

Be comforted, my dear, and let Christ be exceedingly precious to your soul, never doubting his love. 'Unto us therefore which believe he is precious.'

The Lord be with thee, my dear daughter, and sustain thee.

My love to you and to all the saints,

John Metcalfe

Temple Orchard,
High Wycombe,
Buckinghamshire.

Miss Lee Lye Sim,
Singapore 1336.   2.2.88

My dear Lye Sim,

GRACE be unto you, mercy, and peace, from God our Father, and the Lord Jesus Christ.

I was so glad to get my daughter's letter, telling me of the kindness and love of a Saviour who has provided for her, leading her to a place of employment according to her prayers. All these providences of God, all the answers

50

to prayer, in our pilgrimage, serve to show the love of the Father, the grace of the Saviour, and the sending forth of the angels to do his bidding in opening doors of opportunity to the child of God.

Thus, such providences, such answers, are to be stored up and treasured, as so many tokens of his love who is invisible, but whose love has thus been made visible.

And yet these, valuable as they are, are but nothing compared to the heavenly, spiritual, and divine provision inwardly ministered in Christ by the Holy Ghost through the word of God. Not in outward providences—valuable, I say, as they are—but in inward glory, the witness stands. Not that your name is written on the role of employees—answer to prayer though it is — but that your name is written in heaven, is the cause of true and abiding rejoicing.

The work in the heart, Lye Sim, my daughter, the work in the heart. It is slow, painful, accompanied by much travail and affliction, yes, yet here is found the being made conformable to his image. To know him, to know the power of his resurrection, the fellowship of his sufferings, and to be made conformable unto his death, if by any means we might attain unto the resurrection of the dead: here is our real business on earth. At this time for you, accompanied by a beneficial providence.

Yet, at another, all your providences will run against you, there will be the hiding of his countenance, the heavens will be as brass, his ear shut, and all will appear to testify that you are forsaken: these are the best times! Here are the times that enlarge the heart, make room for the Spirit, mortify the flesh, provide fire to try faith, and, at the last, endured, yield the peaceable fruit of righteousness unto them that are exercised thereby.

Yet how kind and understanding is the Father! For, when we need it most, then heaven seems to smile, his ear is open, his countenance seen, the way is clear, all opens before us, and we go on full of love and praise. Treasure it up, my dear, treasure it up. Storms are yet to come, when you will be glad to open the treasury, and bring forth the comfortable memories of bygone times: then, then these present favours will comfort you. Yet the mark of his love in the storm is greater than the mark of his love in the time of tranquillity. Only, it does not seem so to our frailty at the time.

In all things and circumstances rejoice in Christ. Be inward. Be deep. Avoid superficiality, and a material outlook, like the plague. Keep your eyes on the Lord, pant earnestly after him, cherish the influences of the Spirit, look to be filled with the Holy Ghost, lightened by the hope set before you, a pilgrim and a stranger upon the earth on the way to glory.

Now may God and our Father bless my daughter, whom I love dearly in the truth.

You are ever on my heart and in my prayers,

John Metcalfe

Lee Lye Sim

Temple Orchard,
High Wycombe,
Buckinghamshire.

Miss Lee Lye Sim,
Singapore 1336.   15.1.89

My very dear daughter in Christ,

GRACE be unto you, mercy, and peace, from God
our Father, and the Lord Jesus Christ.

Your very welcome letter came yesterday, and I want
you to know that my heart was touched at the kindness
and love expressed to me. I know that such expressions
do not come easily to you, and that you never speak
lightly of your interior feelings: it humbles me to know
that I have your love and confidence as an elder and
father in Christ, and by grace I trust and hope to serve
you faithfully in all the things pertaining to the faith of
Christ, and to the house of God, so long as I live.

The older one gets the more change one sees in things
one hoped were at least stable, if not immutable. But
neither this stability nor this immutability shall ever be
found on earth, in earthly things, in what is visible, or
from that which is born of the flesh. The tragedy and
awful disillusionment is that this seems to apply equally,
if not more, to the 'church', and to those that profess
Christ's name.

53

But I trust, yea, yearn, that you shall find heavenly and divine things established by the grace of God in my ministry which will reflect the only stability, immutability, and certainty that exist in this world or the next, in time or eternity: that is, in the Rock of our salvation.

Since you have decided to leave so soon, despite the provision, at least do please take care in your next choice of employment. It was in my mind that perhaps a good bank—preferably Western—might suit you? I say Western, not because I prefer Western things, or think them better, but because I understand that the terms of employment, and the consideration for employees, are more favourable in that connection. I follow your course with interest and concern. Nevertheless, the LORD will guide you and direct your pathway.

Now I must close. My love abides with you, and of my care and constancy you may be assured.

Ever yours in the grace of our Lord Jesus Christ,

John Metcalfe

Lee Lye Sim

Temple Orchard,
High Wycombe,
Buckinghamshire.

Miss Lee Lye Sim,
Singapore 1024.   2.8.89

My dearly beloved Lye Sim,

GRACE be unto you, mercy, and peace, from God
our Father and the Lord Jesus Christ.

I feel so sorry not to have replied to your letter, but,
whilst I am writing, I give myself wholly to that work.
Literally, I am at my labour from early morning—rising
very early—till late at night, seven days a week, shut up
entirely to this one thing. When I finish, I am exhausted.

Then unanswered letters stare me in the face. But I am
so washed out that like the priest and the Levite I pass
by on the other side, leaving my poor letters bruised and
battered across the road. I must be a Jew. I cannot be a
Samaritan. Woe is me! Now therefore legal conscience
goads me, and I take up my pen to write these words:
Sorry I have not written.

I trust this will suffice by way of pouring in oil and wine,
and taking up your battered missive on the back of my
own beast, carrying it to the inn of this brief and simple
explanation, where I hope it will find rest.

But my love is unchanged, and I remember you constantly before the throne of grace with thanksgiving and daily intercession.

Ever yours in the grace of Christ,

John Metcalfe

LEE KAM YEN

PASTORAL LETTER TO
Lee Kam Yen

Taman Serasi,
Singapore.

Miss Lee Kam Yen,
Singapore.   7th month, 1985.

Kam Yen, Although I am now in Singapore, and although I might as easily speak with you face to face, still, your letter to me in England has been sent to me here, and when you phoned me last night you asked me to answer, so I will fulfil your request.

FIRST. You thought I was proud. You could not believe me to be a man of God. You could not suppose that God should send such a person. Kam Yen, this gives me no offence, nor do I mind your saying these things, for my own part. If I were not as nothing in my own sight; had I not a broken and contrite heart: were I not but an empty vessel, helpless and inert of itself, then, then I might be offended. But I am not offended.

What do you expect me to say? That I am not proud? That I am sent? I shall not say these things, nor attempt to dissuade you from your opinion: 'If I bear witness of myself, my witness is not true.' 'To the law and to the testimony: if they speak not according to this word, it is because there is no light in them.'

The truth is, Kam Yen, what lies behind your view of myself, is your unbelief that so great a God could or would do ANYTHING that involved his stooping to men in general, and to this people in particular. Your view of the Almighty is of a Being so remote, so high, so incomprehensible, so incommunicable, so far removed from this world and mankind, that it is inconceivable that he should actually stoop down and really involve himself in the affairs of men, making himself known, and expressing his own will.

But you are quite wrong, Kam Yen: your view is that of man's religion, and not of God's revelation. 'But to this man will I look, saith the LORD, even to him that is poor, and of a contrite spirit, and trembleth at my word.' And again, 'The tabernacle of GOD is'—mark that, Kam Yen, IS; not, 'will be'—'with men, and he will dwell with them.' Once more, Psalm 113:5,6, 'Who is like unto the LORD our God, who dwelleth on high, Who humbleth himself to behold the things that are in heaven, and in the earth!'. And, Kam Yen, besides all this, 'The WORD was made flesh, and dwelt among us, (and we beheld his glory,) full of grace and truth.'

This is he who sent his servants, and why should Kam Yen suppose that he has ceased to send them now? The only reason is, unbelief. Believe not on me, Kam Yen, God forbid: but believe on HIM, and believe in his love for you. Personally.

As to faith, it will soon dispel your unbelief. How should you gain faith? 'Faith cometh by hearing, and hearing by the word of God.'

The rest of your letter is taken up with the meticulous care you show to be truly sincere, and wholly honest with yourself, and to me. This I value deeply, and give you my assurance of my prayers and careful attention to your spiritual welfare. But this I say; It is upon the Lord Jesus, and in the gospel of free grace, that you must fix your eyes, and in which must lie your heart's delight and meditation: 'then thou shalt make thy way prosperous, and then thou shalt have good success.' That is, in the things of the Spirit.

Be encouraged, my dear Kam Yen: the word is nigh thee, and the name of the Lord Jesus Christ brings all heaven into reach, and inclines the ear of the Almighty, even the God and Father of our Lord Jesus Christ, to hearken to the whispers, sighs, and longings of one so little in her own sight as my dear Kam Yen.

The LORD be thy light,
and thy salvation,
is the prayer of thine to serve, for Christ's sake,

John Metcalfe

LOH SOOK KENG

THE TESTIMONY OF
Loh Sook Keng

Singapore,

10.6.90

Dear Mr. Metcalfe,

THANK you very much for the words of grace ministered to our souls, and at such needful hours too. My heart has been greatly comforted by the consolations in Christ Jesus. Truly I had despised the word of God in all my slothfulness in imbibing the doctrine of Christ which is able to build us up in the most holy faith—often giving the excuses that they are deep. Yet they are the very milk that builds up the infants into young men and fathers.

Mr. Metcalfe, thank you for the book 'The Church: What is it?'. Reading it is so edifying. Such revelations and body of truth, so mightily set forth. What thankfulness to be delivered from denominationalism, what mercies to be gathered under the headship of Christ into his *ecclesia* and what repentance, knowing very well

65

of my contributions to the very ruin and desolation of the professing church, but what comfort that despite the fallen Christendom, Christ will build his *ecclesia* and the Spirit will have his habitation among the saints.

As I pondered over the immensity of God's love and considered what he had done to his Son at Golgotha for me, wretched and born in sin to a fallen race, under the curse of the law, what joy and thankfulness filled my heart. Truly God is my salvation and my light. With a mighty arm has he delivered me from the captivity of the prince of the power of the air, from the bondage of the law and from the body of death.

I was brought up in a traditional Chinese family in a poor 'kampong'. Life was hard, with no material comforts, hardly any electricity or fresh water, and with poor sanitation. The 'kampong' folks were mostly illiterates who reared poultry and pigs or worked as manual labourers. Their only consolation in life was in their strong belief in idolatry. Their dreams of prosperity, fame, and a better present life, their needs of safety and well-being lay in their deep superstition in the powers of their 'gods'. So was my belief as ingrained in me from a little child, subjected to the same powers that blind the heart in the children of disobedience. But praise be to God for his everlasting mercy, I was not left to my destruction!

The first truths of existence and death came when I was only a child. I remember distinctly one morning, awakening from my sleep, I stared at the blue heavens trying to fathom what it was like to be non-existent after death. Where would my being rest? The cycles of life and death, judgment and reincarnation according to the Chinese beliefs frightened me. Stories of people on their deathbed being hauled off in chains by spirits of the underworld haunted my mind. The deep interior bondage of fear drove my darkened heart into idolatry even at such a young age. I also had strange hallucinations of flames of fire whenever I had a fever. My mother, alarmed at my terrified cries, tried various means to cure me of my fears. She sought many 'gods', burnt joss paper and made me drink the ashes—but all to no avail.

When I started school at the age of seven, my fears subsided which I attributed to the safe protection of my 'idol'. I excelled in piety among my siblings, cheerfully carrying out all kinds of errands for the dumb idols under my mother's instructions. However the visions of flames of fire still hounded me at times whenever I came across tracts on judgment or the lake of fire, thrown in the rubbish dump at the backyard. Though I could not read, the pictures and illustrations were enough to shake my soul. Concealing my fears, I would pray to my idols and dead ancestors for forgiveness of all my evil misdeeds, even for those I had not committed but for a later date. Thus was my conscience eased when I committed them later. Such was the wickedness and deceitfulness of my heart.

One day in school about the age of thirteen, my classmates were discussing about religion. For the first time, I heard about the power of God and the name of Jesus in delivering someone oppressed by evil spirits. All I ever knew were the powers of demons and spirits. That higher power filled me with awe and reverence. Yet there was some kind of peacefulness, cleanness, and goodness about it. Definitely not fear! Comparing my outward form of piety, I felt unclean: rebellious, obstinate, rude, vicious, cruel, cold—as I was often reprimanded. My years into my teens were very depressing. I felt lost and insecure about life but this was often misunderstood as 'growing up'. But I sought the higher powers with renewed fervour —especially for peace in the inmost heart.

Roman Catholicism became an attraction for me, being much influenced through the convent school I was attending. At the closing year of fourteen, I wanted to embrace it but had no courage. I had not confided in anyone and felt so lost, not knowing anything more than a few prayers recited each day at school. Besides I had an inexplicable fear whenever I looked at the statue of Mary—similar to my mystical idols.

My decision about Roman Catholicism was put off when I was involved in some bible correspondence. There were booklets of the four gospels (Authorized Version) sent. These I really treasured as I had no bible and they did give me some knowledge of Christ. At fifteen, I yearned to join some church meetings as I had finished my courses.

My first 'church' meeting was at a prayer/fellowship meeting in an 'Assembly of God' shophouse, invited by one of my classmates. I was so thrilled and overjoyed. But to my horror, though warned beforehand, I found myself in the midst of a people (youngsters) wailing and weeping in utter gibberish (unknown 'tongues'). They sounded like mediums in a trance. Confused and frightened, hardly knowing what to do, I vowed never to return again. But that incident did not deter me from seeking for the truth.

It was then that I was brought to my first bible study in a 'mission' church near my school. The 'mission', after all that I had encountered, seemed very serious and 'disciplined'—no frivolity! I was baptized there and for the next nine years was faithfully giving myself to serve God in whatever way I could. In all, I was 'zealous'. Feeling ignorant, I was out almost every night during the week days attending evening meetings, whether they be fellowship, prayer, 'doctrinal' classes, and even biblical Chinese and Greek classes. I was taught about the errors of other denominations, the importance of separation, and to contend for the faith. I even went round distributing tracts and pamphlets to other 'churches' about their errors!

Trouble began with the 'mission' church, and soon they were all taken away and scattered into small groups, meeting in houses of their converts. As time passed, I began to feel very burnt out and weary. Fear gripped me and many questions arose in my mind as I watched enthusiastic youths come one after the other, only to fall away as they got older.

Reading of conversions of godly men and women of the past troubled me. My life had not changed, though my religion had. I felt I was not converted. Rebellion began to rise as the commandments came heavily upon me. They seemed so heavy to bear and each day the same confessions had to be made over again.

Finally convinced that God was wroth and had forsaken me, I broke down and wept and groaned for days. My soul refused to be comforted. Nobody seemed to understand my condition. Nobody cared for my soul. One of the missioners, under whose group I was placed, instructed me to believe and not succumb to my feelings. My heart was neither convinced nor comforted but I submitted to his 'authority'.

However grace at such a dark hour was whispered to me when I read Jn. 11:25,26 one morning. It struck me so deeply though I felt I had no faith to believe at that time. Nevertheless it brought me much consolation.

My heart was heavy when I went to Penang Hill Conference in the twelfth month, 1984, with one motive—to seek God. There I heard you preaching, Mr. Metcalfe, on Psalm 11 and Romans 3:28. What joy! what a difference from the dryness of the dead letter! What refreshing of the Spirit! Though I could not understand all that was preached, yet my spirit could testify that this was indeed the pure word of God. It was this same inexplicable testimony within that constrained me to continue to attend your preaching later on in Singapore.

As light came from the gospel, there followed resistance to that glare from the flesh. Confusion set in. The legality of the teaching I had embraced was brought into question and the shaking to the very foundation of all that I thought I once knew. I saw the hypocrisies of the whole system from the 'elders' on the platform, to the least in the pews—the hirelings who so craved for authority and power now obviously appearing without either call or unction for the ministry, under legal bondage themselves, pretending to be called, yet with not one of their works established by God. No wonder their fruit never did remain—young people came and went and those few older ones who stayed were surely the congregation of the dead.

Though under your ministry much was brought to light, yet there remained the old self that was yet to be broken. The external profession of the letter was a strong cover up. What was not yet discovered was the total

---

depravity of the old nature. Flesh and blood cannot enter the kingdom of heaven. Though religion could change the outward form of doctrine and practice, yet the interior remained untouched. From idol worshipping to Roman Catholicism, to the various sects and denominations, under the law and even into the gospel light—faith cannot be wrought with the will of the flesh. Salvation must be from the LORD alone. He must illuminate the heart, and remove the veil that so blinds the mind and understanding.

I remained about five years under your ministry in the Far East, yet deep within my heart, I knew I was not converted. I was still under the law inwardly, although under the gospel outwardly. The legal spirit remained, and hence I was kept in bondage to the body of sin. What had been nourished under the law in terms of righteousness, judgment, discernment, fleshly ability, all slowly faded away. I was shocked at myself when anger, bitterness, weariness, all manner of evil imaginings and concupiscence broke out. The LORD was showing me my total depravity. How I had not looked to a Saviour outside myself and to him who was crucified and who bore the judgment of God's wrath and put away sin once and for all.

I saw my true state in the twelfth month, 1989, as you spoke of my condition by the mercies of God. I was glad that it all came out. Something which I could never dare admit and would have continued in until I would have been found out in the last day. What grace! What everlasting mercies and longsuffering from God! What kindness to be brought to the light, not of self under condemnation, but of Christ our justification!

On the 26th of the second month, 1990, we had a tape on Romans 10:4-13. Your words spoke exactly what my unbelieving heart would want to say—that is 'Say not in thine heart, Who shall ascend into heaven? (that is, to bring Christ down from above:) Or, Who shall descend into the deep? (that is, to bring up Christ again from the dead.)'. I realized that I had been waiting for something spectacular to happen and had not taken hold of the word of faith that had been sent and preached.

Then I cried to the Lord Jesus as he had been revealed to me in the gospel, and for the first time I saw the light that shines from heaven! I believed on his name to save me; I could do no other: I knew I was liberated. My spirit was set free. I felt the presence of God and his communion and peace filled my soul.

O, Mr. Metcalfe, how I do give thanks to God for his longsuffering—not willing that any of his sheep should perish but that all should come to repentance. How I do give thanks to him for sending his servant to bring in that gospel without which there is no salvation.

Thank you also for all your patience and longsuffering in ministering the word of life and for all your travails in prayer. O may the LORD restore the years that the locusts have eaten, the cankerworm, and the caterpillar, and the palmerworm, and bring to fruition the works of his hands.

Unto him that loved us, and washed us from our sins in his own blood, and hath made us kings and priests unto God and his Father; to him be glory and dominion for ever and ever. Amen.

Your daughter
begotten through the gospel,

Sook Keng

PASTORAL LETTERS TO
Loh Sook Keng

John Metcalfe Publishing Trust,
Church Road, Tylers Green,
Penn, Buckinghamshire.

Miss Loh Sook Keng,
Singapore 2159.   19.2.85

John Metcalfe, a slave of Jesus Christ, and an elder, to
Sook Keng, beloved and faithful sister in Christ:
Grace to thee, mercy, and peace, from God our Father
and the Lord Jesus Christ.

I THANK my God upon every remembrance of thee,
as I do of your sisters in Christ, who have brought
me great consolation and comfort in the Holy Ghost, in
the bowels of Jesus Christ, being much encouraged by
your obedience to the word of God, and strong resolution
neither to turn to the left hand of corruption, nor to the
right hand of error.

Faithful is he which calleth you, who will surely keep your feet from falling and grant your heart's desire: 'Thine ears shall hear a word behind thee, saying, This is the way, walk ye in it, when ye turn to the right hand, and when ye turn to the left.' Moreover, the Lord speaketh unto thee by David, saying, 'Return unto thy rest, O my soul; for the Lord hath dealt bountifully with thee. For thou hast delivered my soul from death, mine eyes from tears, and my feet from falling. I will walk before the Lord in the land of the living.'

Of all that you have told me I have taken careful note, as I have of that which was said in the letter from the other sister. You may be sure of my total confidence. Many of the things you say, the Lord himself had shown me in my heart whilst still in Singapore. Though many have failed you, by the mercy and grace of God, I have been kept faithful, and will be faithful, through being kept of a broken and contrite spirit that trembleth at his word; and through the manifold openings of heart, enlargements of spirit, enlightenments of mind, and blessed seasons of communion, which spring from an inward and heartfelt union with the Father and the Son.

My fruit, to the glory of the Father, remains, and with me are many faithful brethren and sisters, begotten through mine own ministry. So that you may, because of the grace of Father, Son, and Holy Ghost, and the word of God dwelling within, you may indeed feel confidence and trust in me, in the Lord Jesus. And this I say, not that you should think me anything, God knoweth, but for your sakes I say it, because from the depth of my pity and compassion for you all in your confusion I feel your need of someone whom you can trust, that will give a true reflection of the good shepherd, that great shepherd, even our Lord Jesus Christ.

Some boast arrogantly, cutting themselves off from all authority that is in Christ. Oh, say they, 'The LORD is my shepherd.' Forgetting that they are quoting a chosen vessel, David, who wrote this for the comfort of his people. We do need those whom the Lord sends, as did Israel of old. And hence, 'He chose David also his servant, and took him from the sheepfolds: from following the ewes great with young he brought him to feed Jacob his people, and Israel his inheritance. So he fed them according to the integrity of his heart; and guided them by the skilfulness of his hands.'

Here then are two errors into which men may fall: On the one hand, false shepherds, the hirelings, who flee when the wolf cometh. You may see clearly who did that, in Singapore, and when, whatever excuse was given! And, as is the father, so are the children. They too, would flee in their turn, once danger threatened. Very rightly you have judged and forsaken them. The second error, is presumption. To suppose we can dispense with those Davids, Pauls, Peters, and Johns, whom the Lord sends to 'Feed my sheep; feed my lambs', who are to 'feed the flock of God which is among you'. Those who would dispense of these lift up themselves, and lord it over God's heritage, and are not to be trusted. On the contrary, we are to flee from them.

In a broken, dark day like this, when confusion reigns, and when you have been led erroneously, under law and bondage, the Lord has sent you deliverance by the truth of the gospel. Rare indeed is a faithful ministry.

But I do trust that 'Ye have judged me to be faithful to the Lord.' My longing is to comfort your heart, to console you, and to encourage you with all my being in the consolations of Christ. To that end, I am both humbled and overjoyed at the confidence and trust of your letter. You will not find it misplaced.

As I have begun, so I purpose to continue, in faithfulness to Christ's true disciples in Singapore and Malaysia. You will not find me of double mind. 'My heart is fixed, my heart is fixed.' And this is all his grace. And not over a few days, but over many, many years, having waded through seas of affliction, passed over rivers of tribulation, and endured nearly unbearable sufferings, for the word of God and the testimony of Jesus. As many here can bear witness. Now I rejoice that I may be for your consolation and comfort 'A pattern to them which should hereafter believe.' Indeed, with a good conscience, and a true heart, in the glorious gospel of the blessed God, by the Spirit I can say, 'Be ye followers of me, even as I also am of Christ'.

And what shall I advise you? To be prudent, to speak fully and openly only to those sisters of whom you tell me, and to me, myself, for the time being. Not to commit yourself wholly to any, but to keep the counsels of your heart before the Lord, waiting in prayer, alone and with your sisters, and humbly and brokenly pouring out your hearts to the Lord: 'Ye people, pour out your heart before him: God is a refuge for us.'

And to pray for what? My dear daughters, pray, I entreat and beseech you, for the Lord to open the way for me to return, and to build up and establish the work of God among his own people in Singapore. Pray for that, indeed, and pray with humility and faith.

Now, it is the time for the trial of your faith. Let the Lord see your love and confidence in him, and the prudence of your walk in the Holy Ghost. My heart and my spirit take every single step, every movement on the path, together with you, even as if I were there in the flesh.

Take courage: my great love to you all in Christ Jesus.

The grace of our Lord Jesus Christ be with you,

John Metcalfe

Temple Orchard,
High Wycombe,
Buckinghamshire.

Miss Loh Sook Keng,
Singapore.   6.7.87

My Dear Sook Keng,

GRACE be unto thee, mercy, and peace, from God our Father and the Lord Jesus Christ. You must forgive me that I did not reply to your last letter: it does not mean that I do not greatly value and appreciate your letters, it means that I am writing a book. And you know that this is a spiritual travail, more prolonged, more painful, and more enduring than natural travail. If so, you can hardly expect a letter during such labour as that! But then you are getting one now, between pangs as it were, that is, between the eleventh and twelfth chapters, and I know that, with your customary love and understanding, you will sympathize in this work.

Your letter was very welcome, and, as always, spiritual and stable. How encouraging this is. Every day I pray for you, and constantly you are in my mind. I know that you have much affliction and weakness in the body but, blessed be God, you never complain, and you never show this to others.

But the Lord knows your frame, he remembers that you are dust, he does not suffer you to bear above what you are able, and his strength is made perfect in weakness. Oh, where would we be without such chastenings, and reminders of our mortality? What has he kept us from by such all-wise dealings, by which otherwise we would, in our health and prosperity, have destroyed ourselves?

I will bless the Lord at all times, his praise shall continually be in my mouth. The Lord hath chastened me sore, yes, but he hath not given me over to death. 'We have the sentence of death in ourselves, that we should not trust in ourselves, but in God which raiseth the dead: who delivered us from so great a death, and doth deliver: in whom we trust that he will yet deliver us; ye also helping together by prayer for us, that for the gift bestowed upon us by the means of many persons thanks may be given by many on our behalf.'

Now please forgive my brevity. I must begin to consider the next chapter, although as yet I have another, final, revision on the present one. Also, many letters have accumulated, which I must answer. Do pray much for me.

My love to you in the Lord, my dear,

Yours in Christ,

John Metcalfe

Temple Orchard,
High Wycombe,
Buckinghamshire.

Miss Loh Sook Keng,
Bethany Meeting Hall,
Singapore 1129.   23.2.88

My very dear Sook Keng,

YOU know that the Lord meant it for good, to ease your burdens. You know how the Adversary misrepresents him, but in truth it is his delight to comfort all that mourn; to appoint unto them that mourn in Zion, to give unto them beauty for ashes, the oil of joy for mourning, the garment of praise for the spirit of heaviness.

For this cause the Spirit of the Lord GOD is upon him, and it is the reason for which he is anointed: to preach good tidings to the meek; to bind up the broken-hearted, to proclaim liberty to the captives, and the opening of the prison to them that are bound.

See therefore in him One altogether different from the miserable picture painted by the Deceiver. See in him the end of the legal rule, of the dead letter, of the system of touch not, taste not, handle not, of the keeping of days, of the old rigour, of the oft washing, of the continual striving, of the narrow look, the suspicious, censorious, condemnatory spirit, of the traditions of man, which set at nought the word of God.

See! Thy king cometh unto thee: not thou unto him. Meek, and lowly, and riding upon an ass: not furious and indignant, and appearing in a flame of fire. Thou hast not chosen him, but he has chosen thee and, at that, in the furnace of affliction, a sure mark of God's elect. Thou hast not found him, he has found thee, 'I was found of them that sought me not.'

And wherefore? That thou mayest praise his name. Praise for unending, free, unmerited love, love made known in full, everlasting justification, love made known in eternal redemption, love that is strong as death, love that will never let thee go, love that gives an irrevocable pardon world without end. Is not this the best wine? Then drink to the full.

I know that you are very weary, and I know that this is deep in thy bones. Still 'That the bones which thou hast broken may rejoice', wilt thou not repose on his everlasting love? Lay down your burden, give up your strength, let go upon the might of his arm. Saith he, Come unto me, all ye that are weary, and heavy laden, and I will give you rest. Underneath are the everlasting arms. Rest on them then. Rejoice in the Lord, and again I say, Rejoice.

Do not think I am preaching to you, or emptily adding word to word: this is what the Lord, who loves you dearly, would bring to you: not words, but oil and wine. Not exhortation, but rest itself. I beg you, that your joy may be full, that you will wholly open to him, that he may sup with you and you with him henceforth for evermore.

This is not to say that you have not attained to much. You have. It is not to imply that he does not know what this pathway has cost you. He knows full well the price of every step of your true faithfulness.

It is not to say that he is not aware of your purpose of heart, when there seems so little strength for such a great way, so little energy for so vast a toil. He knows. Hence 'Jesus himself drew near.' Believe me, for your comfort, for your strength, for your joy, he delights to pour in oil and wine, to take all the weight, to provide all the energy, to assume every responsibility.

And why? Because 'I have loved thee with an everlasting love.' Rest, rest and joy in that love, I do with all my desire entreat you.

May the LORD bless my dear Sook Keng,
with every grace and a sight of the glory,
and with the love of thy servant,

John Metcalfe

Temple Orchard,
High Wycombe,
Buckinghamshire.

Miss Loh Sook Keng,
Singapore 2366.   26.7.88

My very dear Sook Keng,

YOUR letter has been much on my mind, and I wish to assure you that I pray daily and fervently for you, that grace, mercy, and peace may be multiplied to you in the inward, experimental, and comforting spiritual knowledge of God, and of our Saviour Jesus Christ.

I feel immensely for you in your long and debilitating trials and afflictions, often thinking of you in your place of work. I remember as yesterday, down to minute details, being taken by you to consult your boss, and the kindness shown to me, and the circumstances and environment in which you pass so much of your time.

However, I can say honestly that in the love of Christ I feel the things you describe constantly upon my heart, and your deliverance, or, at least, alleviation and maintenance of balance are as continuously borne up in prayer in my spirit.

Forgive me for not spending longer at this time. Although some progress has been made for good, my case drags on and on, though very well represented. There is not a shadow of doubt about the justice of my cause.

Besides all this, many other burdens, yokes, and trials abide me, some, of course, being the things that obtain in Singapore.

My dear, please forgive my brevity: but believe me, you are on my heart, to live and to die with you, in the love of God, the grace of our Lord Jesus Christ, and in the communion of the Holy Ghost.

To my beloved daughter in Christ
I send my love in the Spirit, and pray
the comfort of the Holy Ghost.

Ever yours,

John Metcalfe

SEAH LAY HUAT

PASTORAL LETTERS TO

Seah Lay Huat

John Metcalfe Publishing Trust,
Church Road, Tylers Green,
Penn, Buckinghamshire.

Miss Seah Lay Huat,
Singapore 0105.   12.1.88

My very dear Lay Huat,

I AM so thankful to the LORD for the blessing that is
upon you. Cherish and lay up these moments when the
clouds pass over, all heaven smiles upon you, whilst the
beams of the Sun of Righteousness light up and illuminate
your soul, to assure and console you with the love of God.
This is the love that can never alter.

The face of heaven can alter. The clouds can gather
again thick over your head, the darkness can come down,
the rain can lash you, the storm can roar, the thunder roll,
and the lightning flash and strike. But 'I have loved thee
with an everlasting love.' 'I have loved you, saith the
LORD.' Nothing can ever alter or change that. Once shown,
it is for ever. Neither can anything alter him, any more

than his love, who is far above the clouds, who is over the heaven of heavens, who at such a time as this has shown you his love, and espoused your heart. 'I am the LORD, I change not.'

He has shown you his love. For you. It is everlasting, unchangeable. You are his child. Oh! Let us bless his name together! He will never leave you, whom he has begotten, nor forsake you. But, sooner or later, the time will come again when your faith must be tried in the storm. This too is a mark of the child. Then, remember his wonderful love which he has shown you now, love that can never change, love which is revealed in your sacrificial Substitute at the cross, love which shall endure for ever. Remember, no storm exists or can exist which can alter that: 'Who shall separate us from the love of Christ?'

Storms are infinitely beneath his wonderful love, his unchangeable love, who is far over all. How strongly I feel that love for you, which he bears to his children, his elect. How blessed you are, dearly beloved Lay Huat, and how grateful, how thankful, how glad I am that it is so.

Set down the blessing in a book of Remembrance, whilst the sense of it is felt by you. Not that anything later can add to or subtract from his love. But the memory of what you have felt now will be greatly for your comfort in a day of darkness to come.

You are predestined for Zion, by the word of a King, by the command of the Almighty, by the will of the Everlasting, dearest daughter, and my heart melts with joy to know that it is so. Do you recall speaking to me that evening in the study at Taman Serasi? I do. All your desires he has granted. Praise ye the LORD.

The LORD bless thee out of Zion, my dear, 'Every one of them in Zion appeareth before God.'

Yours in everlasting love,

John Metcalfe

Temple Orchard,
High Wycombe,
Buckinghamshire.

Miss Seah Lay Huat,
Singapore 1024.   9.4.90

My dear Lay Huat,

GRACE be unto thee, mercy, and peace, from God our Father, and the Lord Jesus Christ.

Thank you for the card you sent me in the second month, Lay Huat: it is where I can see it, in my letter rack, just to one side of my desk.

I continue to remember you in my prayers daily, never forgetting to give thanks to God and the Father, through

Jesus Christ our Lord, for the grace that he has shown you. I know that he heard your cry, and that you are accepted in the Beloved. I feel the witness of the Spirit that he has set his love upon you.

In response, may your heart ever be open and trusting as a little child, joying in the love of such a Father, who has revealed Christ to you, that you should trust in him implicitly. Not just for earthly protection, guidance, and keeping. That is secondary. But for eternal salvation, present communion, and for the ability to distinguish between the flesh and the spirit, the world and Christ, in your pathway. My love and prayers follow you daily, and, best of all, so do those of your great High Priest above, and of your Comforter below.

And the Lord direct your heart into the love of God, and into the patient waiting for Christ.

My love to you in Christ, and in the Holy Ghost.

Yours in grace,

John Metcalfe

Temple Orchard,
High Wycombe,
Buckinghamshire.

Miss Seah Lay Huat,
Singapore 1024.   28.9.90

My dear Lay Huat,

G RACE be unto thee, mercy, and peace, from God
our Father, and the Lord Jesus Christ.

How very kind of you to think of me, and to write such
an encouraging letter. The texts you quote are most suitable, and I do appreciate your sympathy and kindness,
and assure you that I am comforted by the things that
you have said.

And how touched I am that you should send me such
a remarkable photograph! I cannot recall having seen a
picture of a waterspout, and this is is such a fine—indeed,
dramatic—portrayal. I shall treasure this, you may be sure,
the more so because I know that it meant much to you,
and that it was something you valued.

Of course immediately I saw the picture the text sprang
to my mind, just as you quoted it in your letter: 'Deep
calleth unto deep at the noise of thy waterspouts.' The
deep of the heavens above calls to the deep of the waters
below, and the deep of the waters beneath answers to
the deep of the heavenly glory, when God sends forth that
powerful, mighty, upsurging which, at the sound of his

voice, draws up what is below into the very heavens themselves, yet unites the two in the strong pillar of a vital spiritual communion.

How this speaks of the work of the Spirit having revealed the gospel of Christ to the deeps of the heart, at the sound of the word of God elevating all that is in the heart, mysteriously drawing up all that is within into a heavenly communion with Christ on high in the glory, bringing both into the bonds of that spiritual union between God the Father and his own children, between heaven and earth, between the Spirit that dwells in us, and him from whom that same Spirit was sent, and all to the glory of Christ. 'And all that is within me, bless his holy name.'

Now your photograph is set in a special place on the bookshelves that face one as one enters my study, so that every day I remember you as I see the picture. Not that I need reminding. Never a day passes, nor a dawn breaks, without your name being carried before God and our Father in prayer, without that I give thanks for the kindness of his love and grace shown to you, and without that I bow my knees for your continual preservation, growth, and increase in Christ, till he comes again. Amen. Even so, Come quickly, Lord Jesus.

You know what I am moved so often in the Spirit to pray over, concerning you, that it should be fulfilled in you, in your life, and in your experience, that I might rise up with thanksgiving at the answer to my request?

'Thou shalt keep them, O LORD'—that is, keep you— 'thou shalt preserve them'—that is, preserve you—'from this generation'—that is, the fleshly generation, the generation that is in Adam by nature, the generation of the worldly, and of the world—'from this generation for ever.'

For ever? Yes, keep and preserve you in Christ till the day you die, till the last day, till the day you rise again in Christ, till the day you enter the world to come in glory with an everlasting inheritance in Christ. For ever. Keep and preserve you for ever.

It is not, You must keep yourself. It is not, You should preserve yourself. It is, Thou, thou, thou shalt keep them. Now, there is salvation, my dearly beloved daughter, and it is all of God, all in Christ, and all of grace. Rest in these words, for the words of the LORD are pure words: as silver tried in a furnace of earth, purified seven times, Psalm 12:6.

Peace be unto thee, my dear Lay Huat,

With my earnest love in Christ,

John Metcalfe

SIE SIOK HUI

THE TESTIMONY OF
Sie Siok Hui

Singapore,

4th month, 1997.

IT has been on my mind to set forth the wonderful and gracious works the Lord has wrought in my life. Truly, my song is 'Bless the LORD, O my soul: and all that is within me, bless his holy name. Bless the LORD, O my soul, and forget not all his benefits: who forgiveth all thine iniquities; who healeth all thy diseases; who redeemeth thy life from destruction; who crowneth thee with loving-kindness and tender mercies', Psalm 103:1-4.

At a very young age, I was somewhat conscious that my family was not normal. My father did not live with us and there were older children from my mother's past. I was not a goodly child, given to stubbornness and perverseness. This, and the misconduct of the older children, caused my mother to be extremely harsh with me. Punishments were severe and frequent. I was subjected to much fear and unhappiness.

School was my escape. Attending a convent school for ten years, the chapel appeared to be a sanctuary. I was drawn to the Roman Catholic religion, and often, in desperation, I would resort thither during my recess, praying, bargaining, for an escape. I dreaded returning home every day.

Aged eleven, my father's diminishing business was wiped out by the outbreak of foot and mouth disease in the cattle which he imported and exported. From changing cars every two to three years, he drove a lorry to manage the business of his acquaintance and that too failed. Quarrels over finance became frequent, adding to the unhappiness.

As I observed the world of adults around me, I was often filled with despair—and questioned the meaning of life. I enjoyed studying but what after it? Career? Family? Then what? The meaningless cycle of events troubled me. At school, we heard often of 'Mother Teresa'. I thought that was the answer—social work—the only purpose one could have for living—save others. I did not see myself as having need of salvation, save out of the misery of my home.

At fourteen, one of my classmates, a Bible-Presbyterian, declared that I was a sinner and would go to hell unless I 'accepted' Jesus. I was furious with her. Some days later, I related this incident to another classmate, an evangelical, who said to me, Jesus loves you—just pray and receive him into your heart. That appealed to me—and that night I did—knowing full well my parents would oppose. But I thought that I need not tell them about it. Thus began my 'profession'—an empty one. I did not attend anywhere for fear of my parents.

Between fifteen and sixteen, my mother suffered from terrible depression and took to drinking. I slept in the same room as her. Some nights were sheer nightmare lasting till almost dawn. Violence was not infrequent. Blasphemy, cursings, and foul language were shouted into the darkness throughout the night. Yet during the day she seemed oblivious that these things had taken place. The darkness and oppression of those moments drove me to call upon the name of the Lord. I cried till I could cry no more and there was none I could turn to for help. My only comfort was that the Lord would take pity on me—and strangely, I felt he did. That was my sole consolation.

Through my classmates, some who were very 'catholic', I learned of the confusion in the Christian faith. I was baffled. Why so many denominations? The answer was, 'All are the same—the only difference is in the manner of worship.' Purgatory was introduced to me by a Seventh-day Adventist and that was a relief to me, to have a second chance. But another told me it is not in the bible. Then evolutionist theory was taught in biology and I was troubled. I was told not to 'give heed to fables and endless genealogies, which minister questions' and that everything must be in accordance with the bible. Everything was debate. There was no knowledge of salvation, much less of the doctrine of Christ.

At seventeen to eighteen, I attended a bible-study group led by a missioner from a fundamental sect connected with the 'Revd.' Ian Paisley, violently anti-Romanist. Billy Graham was in Singapore at that time with the slogan 'I found it' all over public places. Tongue-speaking was another controversial issue. I did not comprehend much nor did I like the militant approach of the sect with which I met, but was altogether put off leaving them by the Billy Graham campaign which I found wholly obnoxious. Attending one tongue-speaking crusade by accident, I was convinced they were emotional, psychological pretensions.

So I experienced, this was wrong, that was wrong—but what was right? Neither was I seeking for that which was just before God, which was in Christ, but rather the things which were of self.

At that time, the first apprehension of fear that I was not truly saved came to me. Was I that bad? Did I need a Saviour to save me? I knew I was wayward and could number the wrongs I had done but somehow it didn't seem that bad. Then I began to feel I should make my profession known at home and take a stand. I was required to burn joss-sticks daily. Buying lottery tickets, beer, and cigarettes was also my duty, as I ran all the errands from home. By that time, my father had come to live with us, and I was delivered from the night tortures. Crippled with fear, I took my stand. The storm raged—and I was not expected to hold out. A brother and sister before me had made this profession but within a short time gave in to pressure, distracted by new events in their lives. So would I have been, had not the Lord laid his hands on me. I realized that 'taking stands', of which so much is made, whilst necessary, is not the basis of true religion at all.

With financial instability at home, I gave tuition to younger children to support my own studies. With a scholarship, and later a bursary, I was enabled to pursue my university education, working every vacation as well.

Tumults continued to rule at home, and it was agreed that it was best for me to stay at the hostel to help me concentrate on completing my course. This was in mid 1980.

I was glad of the decision and genuinely thought that this would mean I would be free to seek the Lord without interference. Little did I know that, for the next two years, I was to discover the plague of my own heart. That this was in me, *in* my being, and *not* in the circumstances which I blamed for my troubles.

With a multitude of activities and organizations at the hostel and university, I deviated from the path that I had set out to pursue in my mind and will. Yet I could not reconcile worldly activities with the Christian faith, and could not bring myself to join the VCF (Varsity Christian Fellowship) who did not seem to have any conflicts about the world. I was questioned by one of their leaders whether I thought no one else could be Christians, save those from fundamental sects. I was not attending anywhere, feeling too foul to do so—I only knew the world and the Lord just cannot be mixed.

Nevertheless, deceived, I wanted to have my own life. I felt like a lost sheep, longing for the Shepherd to leave the ninety-nine to come and rescue me. But I was drawn more and more into the world. I despaired of ever finding the Lord. To make things worse, I gradually got into a relationship with a male student, which from the beginning we knew would end, because he was utterly atheistic, clever but unprincipled. Such is the folly of the flesh. This short four-month entanglement brought me to a complete halt in 1982. My conscience, soul, and spirit were in such turmoil. I failed the examinations and had to repeat the course for another year.

I was in a terrible state. Sleep usually eluded me, and when I did sleep, nightmares haunted me. The university doctor referred me to a visiting psychiatrist who diagnosed the root of my problem as my religious convictions. The bible, he said, was old-fashioned and some things cannot apply now. I knew even then that he was a liar. I was given anti-depressants for a week, and told that would help me. The first I took knocked me out for twelve hours. I woke up in dread, fear, and darkness. I refused to continue the medication. But I did not know how to carry on.

Some kind friends at the hostel persuaded me at that time to join them for worship. I finally agreed. I walked with them to a distance from their destination and it dawned on me to ask if this was a charismatic meeting. It was. I apologized but could go no further with them. Thus I felt the mercy of God upon me to keep me from error despite my disobedience.

On the recommendation of the psychiatrist, I was given three months medical leave. During this time, I worked day and night—for my bursary was suspended—and that year I had not the means to pay the university fees. I did not tell my parents. I would have quit the university altogether were I not in bond by law to complete the course and to serve in teaching for six years. I had not the money to pay the damages incurred if I broke the contract.

I wanted to return to worship, but not anywhere. The fundamentalist mission, with which I began, was by then in trouble with the authorities for their 'School of Mission', which they had used to ensnare the young into 'full-time service'. I did not know where they were meeting. I heard of a reformed church and tried to look them up, but lost my way. I never found them.

Sie Siok Hui

Returning to the university in late 1982 after the period of convalescence, I discovered that the temporal respite could not heal the gaping wound within. There was such pain and deep inward despair. The meaninglessness of everything consigned me to hopelessness. I felt it was pointless carrying on. I can still remember vividly how the verse from I Cor. 10:13 came so powerfully into my soul, 'There hath no temptation taken you but such as is common to man: but God is faithful, who will not suffer you to be tempted above that ye are able; but will with the temptation also make a way to escape, that ye may be able to bear it.' That afternoon I cried to the Lord for mercy, and resolved within myself to seek for the Lord.

The following week, I finally joined the bible-study group held at the university by a fundamentalist missioner from the original group. I was distressed by the messages often. It was no balm to a wounded spirit. Yet I continued on, hoping to find a way to the Lord, hoping to make amends, hoping to be restored to the faith. But the legal whipping persisted, making one feel guilty for the soul of every one to whom one had not testified, insomuch that some of us avoided public transport lest the blood of the strangers we met be upon us if we kept silence. Like a pendulum, my 'faith' swayed. I would have left, feeling I was just no good, not right—and did for a short period in 1983.

I was often not in good health, and persistent pain troubled me. It was diagnosed as 'murmuring' appendicitis and required an operation when it turned acute. That frightened me for I had no one to turn to. Again I did not tell my parents, nor did I have any worldly friends. I returned to the meetings and finally when I admitted myself to the hospital on my own for the operation, I felt more at peace to face it. It was discovered that I had a cyst which was removed and it was to be examined to confirm that it was not malignant. The horror and dread of such a prospect gripped me and I clave to the Lord for mercy, and he did show me mercy despite my sins.

Thereafter, in 1984, I became steadfast in attendance at the meetings and evangelism and was made a 'group leader' over young girls, many of whom were supposed to be called to 'mission' work with less than minimum financial provision. I was often left with meagre income in order dutifully to support them. The emptiness within was yawning. My sins, my very being, were a great weight upon me. Yes, now I could see myself in Romans 7, Psalm 25, Psalms 38, 51, 77, 88, and 143: and there was no relief save a constant pushing to do something.

By the great mercies of our God, we heard of a 'peculiar' preacher from England who had been invited to preach at the 'conference' in Penang in the twelfth month, 1984. There was much discussion about him. By now, this fundamentalist sect was filled with internal strifes and conflicts amongst the leaders. The group I was with was the 'life' of the sect, led by one who delighted in appearing fervent and zealous, and, to further this impression, he adopted a persecution complex.

Hence, when Mr. Metcalfe came preaching—for he was the 'peculiar' preacher—first on I Thess. 1:3-9, then from Psalm 11, this group received with joy the word, seeing themselves to be the ones whose course was right and others persecuting them to be exposed for what they were. But when justification by faith was declared with power, it was too 'Calvinistic' — truly these are the deceitful workers, so aptly described in the epistle of Jude.

But to those of us who were sore broken in our soul and spirit, we received the word with fear, knowing within that we had not answered to the 'turning' described in I Thess. 1:9. The word preached on justification by faith was a comfort to me personally, for I was convinced that in me dwelleth no good thing. Except it be by election, I would be lost. Faith must be the gift of God for try as I might, I could neither please God, nor find him.

I must add, at this point, my first acquaintance with the servant of God. I was sitting on the steps with some much younger girls, when Mr. Metcalfe, who was taking a walk, came toward us. He stooped down and spoke kindly to the children. That kind gesture touched me. There was no distance or pretension about him.

Returning to Singapore, Mr. Metcalfe continued to minister to the people daily and took on public preaching for five nights at Pasir Panjang despite having severe back pain. This labour of love remains a blessing to us to this day through the recorded messages. Though I did not apprehend much at that time, it was clear that the system we were in *bore no resemblance* to the apostolic word delivered. The fundamentalist sect — so-called — was as disobedient, if not more so, than those they condemned. The leaders appeared to receive Mr. Metcalfe wholeheartedly and I almost thought and hoped that there would be a reformation within.

But it was not so.

The day before Mr. Metcalfe left, some of us had the opportunity to meet with him for fellowship. He spoke of many things most spiritual—but I was too carnal to retain his words. Two things I remembered — one, he challenged us to think of the tree of life and the tree of knowledge of good and evil, to think and ponder and not just sit there blankly. He spoke of the doctrine of justification by faith—and I remember asking him, But what of our state: my state which I felt to be so alive, in sin—to which he replied, 'Reckon yourself to be dead indeed unto sin'. In my heart, I cried, But I can't. How? It took me some ten years from thence, when these words which were kept in my heart, came back with power, so that now I can say, Yea, I can, For we are buried with him by baptism into death. I am crucified with Christ.

Barely had Mr. Metcalfe left Singapore in the first month of 1985, than the leaders showed their enmity against the word of truth preached unto them. Soon, the group leader of our 'live' section, seizing the opportunity, used Mr. Metcalfe's name to cause a split, consequently leaving the sect. This was directly against Mr. Metcalfe's counsel.

Claiming to receive Mr. Metcalfe's ministry wholly, and willing to sit under him to learn from him, he led many with him. In his own words, 'this was a recovery beyond that of the Reformation. It was back to the beginning of the apostolic word.' I was relatively 'senior' amongst the sisters and was coerced to attend 'secret' meetings which I felt were not right. Some of us began to write to Mr. Metcalfe and his replies to our letters were our nourishment and comfort during that period of darkness and confusion. A few others left both groups.

Lawless, utterly without fear of God, many of the so-called worship meetings held were blasphemous. The few of us who could not agree with them were treated most unkindly and ostracized by the majority. We would have left, except for the entreaty of Mr. Metcalfe assuring us he would return, and that we should walk peaceably so as not to hurt Christ's sheep amongst the mixed multitude.

During this time, the singing of Psalms, and reading of the Trust books were our meat. I remember how the inward state of my soul was so mirrored in the first two beatitudes opened up in 'The Messiah'. To this day, I remember how shattered I was by these words—'Realism perforce causes the soul to admit its emptiness and deadness. The hollow sham of lying pretence—that was once the mind's defence against the truth of one's true condition—is now entirely deflated and debunked.'

'Providentially, by long pressures and seeming catastrophes, God brings the soul to a halt in which it is made to consider its latter end', 'The Messiah', page 150.

I wept—but felt no comfort. The answer must lie in the gospel. Yet I felt I did not know it for when I read the tract 'The Gospel of God' I was certain that I had no understanding. But yet I believed in Christ who died for me, and rose from the dead.

In God's eternal counsel, he sent his servant back to Singapore in the seventh month, 1985. I could not believe it when I heard it and rejoiced to see his servant again. But the very next day, at the meeting of the man who divided from the fundamentalist sect, claiming to follow Mr. Metcalfe, it was announced that neither he nor they would abide under the authority of the man whom God had sent with his word, but that those amongst them who wished to do so should leave immediately. A remnant of us stood up and left.

How betrayed and hurt the Lord's servant must have felt after a journey of twenty-five hours over thousands of miles. I would never have believed that he could have suffered to stay with us, but such was his pity for the poor flock to which he had ministered by prayer and letter over this time—he abode with us. And thus we found experimentally the difference between a hireling and a true servant of God.

Thus Bethany Meeting Hall came to birth, an amalgam of a few of us from the fundamentalist mission, and another group who had heard Mr. Metcalfe preach. Some who had left these groups were also contacted and informed of the meetings and these joined with us.

There followed six months of labour by Mr. Metcalfe, day and night, to build us up in doctrine and in faith. And what a breaking down was needed, nevertheless he was patient with us, reasoning and preaching from the scriptures to root us out of our false notions, pride, and self-interest. Truly, he travailed as a woman with child to bring forth his spiritual children.

For the first time, we heard of the doctrine of Christ, of righteousness, sanctification, and redemption; of the three distinct Persons of the Godhead; of the eternal Sonship of Christ, his birth, his ministry, his death, his resurrection, and his ascension; of the wonderful works of the Holy Ghost in salvation, in the ministry—and more, so that our faith stand not in the wisdom of man, but the power of God.

As the gospel seed was sown, so it was that the tares of the enemy were secretly scattered abroad. During this time, Mr. Metcalfe was compelled to return to England twice to deal with the false brethren using the evil treachery of his own household that took place in England when his back was turned. There was no respite for the servant of God either in Singapore or the United Kingdom, for the enmity of all the hypocrites was beginning to be unveiled so that what became manifest was the fallen countenance of Cain, and—withal lying malice—the murderous spirit of the Accuser of the brethren.

I remember, on his return from the U.K., we met him at the airport and returned to his apartment where he spoke to us of the one hundred and forty-four thousand that were sealed in Revelation 7. He brought up the significance of the number and the consolation of this passage to the people of God. I was impressed and thought things must be alright in England. When most of the people had left, I saw a glimpse of the pain on his face, and sensed the anguish of his spirit. I realized that what I had supposed was very far from being the case.

I left with a heavy heart knowing that the work of the enemy, so terrible in England, had also begun in Singapore. The next day, the first day of the week, I brought breakfast for the Lord's servant. I saw him in deep soul travail and pain. Deep inside, I wondered how he would be able to deliver the word in but a few hours to come. But deliver it he did from II Cor. 1:20, 'For all the promises of God in him are yea, and in him Amen, unto the glory of God by us.' So powerful, so affirmative, so positive was the word declared, that I can honestly feel the power of that word preached to this day.

These observations I kept in my heart, and know for a truth that this is a servant raised up of God. For none can preach such wondrous things of Christ in so much sore affliction, save the grace and power of God rest upon him. No one hearing him would have known the depth of pain and sorrow in this man of God.

Mr. Metcalfe returned to England in the first month of 1986, and within a month, aided and abetted by apostate backsliders in England, the false brethren amongst us rose up to speak wickedly against the servant of God. Yea, they desired to swallow the little flock whom the Lord in his mercies had gathered. By the reign of the Almighty who gave foresight and wisdom unto his servant, Bethany Meeting Hall was kept and those that were his sheep were gathered under this ministry sent to us of God.

But the evil doers would not rest, and raised subtly a false report — feebly assisted by the nonentities in the U.K. — against the Lord's servant to the authorities, preventing him from entering into the land. But God be praised, though they connived such schemes and lies, the truth and his servant's honour were subsequently vindicated by the mighty hand of God, and he was justified by the same authorities to the shame of the scheming liars who had connived behind his back, being persons not worthy of notice.

Nevertheless in the tumult we were devastated. The oldest amongst us was but twenty-six, most were much younger, and we were all poor. In God's great compassion, we were granted favour to obtain premises for worship, and this kindness was extended to us over a period of seven years in our earthly pilgrimage.

But the Lord would not have half measures, half-heartedness, double-mindedness. He would deal with the root, at the heart. All fallow ground must be broken up, and every false foundation exposed.

I was often troubled when asked for my testimony for I could not say how or when I was converted. Indeed often hearing the word, I could not lay claim on the many promises given to the children of God. Deep in my heart, I feared I was not saved. Yet I did believe and could not deny that Christ died for me, a sinner. The responsibility of keeping the affairs of the meeting amongst the sisters became a heavy burden. I was also entangled again in a relationship with one, supposedly a true brother, whom I knew within myself was not right with God, despite his being a 'missioner' in the past. That added to the multitude of conflicts. In the first month of the year following, he left.

In the twelfth month of 1986, Mr. Metcalfe came to us in Penang and perceived many contrary states amongst us, both in the congregation from Singapore and that in Penang. How it must have broken his heart whilst deep in fiery trials, that he could not rejoice over the fruits of his labours. States were exposed and so was my inward condition. I was sharply rebuked by word and later by letter. I was in a state of turmoil and rebellion and could not subject myself to obedience and discipline. The word preached became condemnation to me and I dreaded every message that denounced sin. Though grace was declared, I heard it not. I could not believe that, having received so much truth, I should be in such a peevish incorrigible state. I felt that I was Esau who found no place for repentance, and like the foolish virgins, I was found out without oil in my vessel.

Finally in 1987, fifth month, I left Bethany Meeting Hall to follow after the erring false brother, an act I am ashamed of to this day, for I forsook my brethren and sisters in the time of their greatest need and sore poverty.

The departure gave me no peace nor respite in the soul. In fact I lost everything, including the relationship. It brought me to the depth of depression and to despair of life itself. I was haunted by the fear of death. Some days I would rush back from school and read the bible for hours in a cold sweat until a calmer state prevailed. At that time, one of my students, to whom in my anguish I had testified of Christ, attended Bethany. Thus I was reminded daily of my rebellion when I saw her. I remember two occasions when I could not continue teaching in the classroom, excused myself and hid in the wash-room, beseeching the Lord on my knees in tears to recover me.

On first days, I wandered aimlessly around, sometimes standing afar to see the saints enter into Bethany. I sneaked in on two occasions to hear the word hoping to find strength to return, but the Lord would not have anything but total repentance, and there was no blessing.

I somewhat regretted severing all worldly ties with friends. I made contacts but, after meeting up with some of them, found the company gave no pleasure whatsoever.

Nothing was right. My mother had a serious operation for perforated appendicitis and was hospitalized three weeks and finance became a problem again. In school, official documents of my students were stolen, and there were anonymous complaints made against me. My principal, an elderly lady, well-disposed to me, was kind and said to me she could not understand why all these things were happening to me. In my heart I answered, Because the hand of the LORD was gone forth against me. Like Naomi of old, I felt that the Almighty had dealt bitterly with me.

In the eleventh month, very unexpectedly, a letter from England arrived. The opening words were:

'My daughter,

'Seek I not rest for thee, that it may be well with thee? You cannot believe that he can still love you, but I believe.'

I could not understand that at such a time so great a token of grace and love would be shown to me. I was touched, very touched, and grateful. But I felt I was more hardened and in a worse state than when I had left. Since I could not better myself, how could I be certain that my state would not surface again. If I returned and defiled others? I had done enough damage. Yet the Lord's servant wrote:

'But your state is incorrigible, impossible, it only gets worse. Yes it does. But it can get nothing but worse, filthier, more truculent, more despairing, more hopeless. Quite so. This is called the flesh. It cannot get better. It cannot be improved. It can only get more corrupt. That is why Jesus bore it into judgment on the tree. But we must live with it. Or rather, reckon ourselves dead to it.'

How true! The flesh cannot get better, only more corrupt. But the Accuser continued to trouble me and tormented me that it would be of no use. I could not accept the cost and it would be a worse damnation. Such was the battle within. I knew not at what date Mr. Metcalfe would be in Penang in the twelfth month nor where, for the meeting place had moved. I was too ashamed to call any of the saints, nor did I dare, lest I defile them. All I had was a phone number of a relative of one of those that met in Penang.

Finally, by the great grace of my God, I was enabled to make a last minute arrangement to fly to Penang on the 28th of the twelfth month, 1987. What if I could not find the new meeting room? What if the Lord's servant had left? What if he discerned that I had taken far too long to come? What if I met with an accident even before getting there? Multitudes of tormenting fears taunted me.

All glory and praise be unto our God and Saviour that this lost wayward sheep was carried back and received into the fold by the good Shepherd and Bishop of her soul. Yea, salvation is altogether of God and a thorough work it is—but all completed by Christ, our Saviour. Yea, the LORD has chastened me sore: but he hath not given me over unto death. It brought to pass the words of his servant in a letter on 20.4.85:

'There is that in you, Siok Hui, which God hath wrought. In very much, it is less than you think. As you are discovering, and this casts you down ... But in much also, this wonderful work of God is much, much more than you think. And this also you shall discover.'

And discover it I did.

Yet the work did not stop there. It was only the beginning. There was much hardness of heart and unbelief.

There was a slowness of heart to receive the doctrine in the inward parts though every word of the truth was embraced. I was inclined to be affected by circumstances and be earthly-minded. For a long time I despaired of this state in me and felt that I would never be healed of such an awful condition. I was counselled to study humility before my brethren, to wait upon the Lord, enduring the hardness. The Lord is not at the beck and call of man who thinks he can choose to call down the Lord when he wants. The Lord reigns over all things and when he would try us, it is impossible to break prison.

When I read Mr. Huntington's reply to Mr. and Mrs. Mercer in 'The Ministry of the New Testament', Vol. 12 No. 1, I was much comforted when he described the work of grace being carried on slowly in some and gradually rising from stage to stage, from strength to strength, till the day dawn, and the day star arise in their hearts. This I found to be my experience. I was to learn that the Lord would not have the flesh and the pride of man in his things. All natural ability must be brought to nought until one is totally dependent on him.

When it was, I cannot quite say. It would be some six to seven years after my return to Bethany. Through manifold trials, afflictions, and chastisements from our gracious Father in heaven, my ears were bored and the word of God came forth with refreshed quickening power. Now his words became spirit and life, and the sole joy of my being. The hardness has been quite broken. In place he has bestowed a sweet yielded spirit of meekness and subjection. The wonderful work and Person of our Lord Jesus Christ prefigured and foretold in the old testament, presented in the four accounts of the gospel, in the epistles, his things, his saints, his *ecclesia*, the work of the ministry now became exceedingly precious.

As to my life, it is not my own. It has been purchased by blood. The self and the affairs of this present life will clamour for attention ever so often, but by the teaching of the Spirit, these are subdued. Not just reckoning oneself dead unto sin, but to be alive unto God through Jesus Christ my Lord.

Now the looking for the return of our Blessed God and Saviour Jesus Christ, the vision of the new heaven and new earth wherein dwelleth righteousness fills me with great joy and hope in believing. The old is passed away.

Yea, what have I left to say?

'And in that day thou shalt say, O LORD, I will praise thee: though thou wast angry with me, thine anger is turned away, and thou comfortedst me. Behold, God is my salvation; I will trust, and not be afraid: for the LORD JEHOVAH is my strength and my song; he also is become my salvation. Therefore with joy shall ye draw water out of the wells of salvation', Isaiah 12:1-3.

Unto him that loved us, and washed us from our sins in his own blood, and hath made us kings and priests unto God and his Father; to him be glory and dominion for ever and ever. Amen.

Sie Siok Hui

PASTORAL LETTERS TO
Sie Siok Hui

John Metcalfe Publishing Trust,
Church Road, Tylers Green,
Penn, Buckinghamshire.

Miss Sie Siok Hui,
Singapore 1024.   7.2.85

John Metcalfe, a servant of Jesus Christ,to Sie Siok Hui,
sister in Christ, and daughter in the Lord:
Grace to you, mercy, and peace, from God our Father and
the Lord Jesus Christ.

MY dear Siok Hui, I feel greatly for you and with you
in all the spiritual exercises through which you are
passing. The people of God, his own elect, are no strangers
to the waters breaking into their soul (Psalm 69:1), the
ground failing beneath their feet (Psalm 69:2) and being
covered with confusion (Psalm 69:7).

Nor is it any new experience to a quickened soul to feel
what you feel within, since it is common to such a poor
people to 'mourn in their complaint, and make a noise'

117

(Psalm 55:2), for their heart 'to be sore pained within them' (Psalm 55:4) and, at the last, 'fearfulness and trembling to come upon them'.

Now, since these are these experiences you describe, of what can you complain? For it is a truth, no Hagarene ever knew these sensations, no bastard shared these chastisements, none of the uncircumcised ever did or will know the least of what you describe. To all that you describe, Cain, Balaam, Saul, Tobiah, Sanballat, Goliath, Esau, Judas, Ananias, Sapphira, and Demas, were and are perfect strangers.

But with these spiritual exercises, to these inward sensations, Abel, Enoch, Noah, Job, Abraham, David, Daniel, Peter, John, and Paul, were all intimately and internally acquainted, sometimes for years together without remission or relief, describing their experiences in various parts of the bible. To these places the Spirit of truth leads us for our comfort and consolation.

Rejoice greatly that you are a partaker of their sufferings, inwardly and outwardly, and not of the hypocrites, concision, dogs, Pharisees, and letter-learned talkers. You have so much to be thankful for, my dear daughter. Rejoice greatly, O daughter of Zion! Arise, shine; for thy light is come, and the glory of the LORD is risen upon thee.

But for the experience of that, you must patiently wait in the obedience of faith. Keep the faith in a good conscience. Meantime trust, even though the path be dark. Trust me also, that I WILL come, but in THE LORD's WILL, not mine, nor yours. Meanwhile, pursue, together with all like-minded brethren, a steady course of obedience, reading, and prayer. And, under the storm, in the dark, TRUST THE LORD. And be assured, he will send help in due time, after your faith is tried, and your obedience proved. 'After ye have suffered a while.' Just a while.

The Lord bless and keep you my beloved daughter. I use your bookmark in the bible by my bedside.

My love in Christ,

John Metcalfe

John Metcalfe Publishing Trust,
Church Road, Tylers Green,
Penn, Buckinghamshire.

Miss Sie Siok Hui,
Singapore 1024.   26.2.85

John Metcalfe, a slave of Jesus Christ, and an elder, to Siok Hui, beloved daughter in Christ:
Grace, mercy, and peace, from God our Father, and the Lord Jesus Christ.

AMIDST labours more abundant, joy was brought to me through my daughter's letter, and I rejoice to hear that you have known the truth, and continue in love to me in the truth, for the truth's sake, which dwelleth in us, and shall be with us for ever.

The Lord has wrought deliverances for Jacob, and will yet deliver his people. Now, you may complain of dryness, which is what no natural man ever did, for none of the carnal, and no hypocrite in Zion, ever yet discovered what it is to thirst, and none ever will.

But my daughter is thirsty. She is dry. Then rejoice, O daughter of Zion, rejoice greatly, for thy King surely cometh unto thee! Who knows what it is to be dry, but the thirsty? Saith the psalmist, I opened my mouth, and panted. Why do you think that was?

All the redeemed of the LORD that ever said so, Psalm 107:2, came but one way, namely, verse 4, 'They wandered in the wilderness in a solitary way; they found no city to dwell in. Hungry and thirsty, their soul fainted in them.' All God's redeemed by Christ Jesus must come this way. As to what satisfied them before, 'He turneth rivers into a wilderness.' As to what shall quench their thirst thereafter, 'He turneth the wilderness into a standing water, and dry ground into watersprings', Psalm 107:verses 33 and 35.

And between these two mighty works of God, in which he dries up all that nature can draw by way of moisture from the law, the gospel, the mind, the affections, and all that is in this world and its religion, and brings the poor, fainting soul from Sinai to Zion, from bondage to liberty, from self-righteousness to everlasting justification, from striving to resting, from labour to peace, from Egypt to the promised land; I say, between these two lies a great waste howling wilderness, and this is that through which you are passing, and must pass.

And think not, that such a great tract of land is crossed in a day, a week, a month, or a year. Ye have need of patience.

Doubt not but, although coming out of Egypt is certainly not entering into the promised rest, nevertheless, no one ever did, no one ever will, nor will such a time ever come to pass, that a people shall be brought of God into the land of promise without the step you have taken in your souls, in departing from iniquity, and leaving the land of your bondage behind.

Say not in thine heart, But how little progress!, or, But I am no better than I was! Rejoice with Miriam and the daughters of Israel on the banks of the Red sea: you are now really pilgrims and strangers; all the hypocrites are spiritually drowned; God hath been a man-of-war for you; the waters parted before your great apostle, Christ Jesus; God is gone up with a shout; a pillar of fire is before you, a pillar of cloud withal: O rejoice greatly, O daughter of Zion! and again I say, rejoice.

Yea, and rejoice in tribulations also. Rejoice in dryness. Who ever from Hagar's children could say, My soul thirsteth for thee? Or, My moisture is turned into the drought of summer? Not one. This is a mark of the elect, not the reprobate.

But and if you say, Yet where are the rivers of water? I reply, In the eye of faith. And if you still answer, But it was not so with Jesus? My response is this, Who said, I thirst? If you say, But what of Paul? My cry is, saith he, I protest by your rejoicing. I die daily!

Rejoice that you are counted among those that are to suffer for that worthy name, and by your joy in the fires of tribulation, to comfort the weak. Do not doubt, your feet shall stand on the banks of Jordan, the ark of God shall go before you, and in due season, if you faint not, you shall stand not only in the promised land, but upon the very mount of Zion. Behold, I, John, say it unto thee! Fear not!

And now, my beloved daughter, my labours claim me again. Faithful is he that hath called you, perfect is that sacrifice. Appeased is thy God and Father. Comforting and comfortable is that blessed Holy Spirit. Trust in him at all times: yea, rejoice in tribulation!

And do you know why I labour day and night, and write to you before the dawn breaks? So that I may finish 'The Hymns of the New Testament', establish the work of publishing, minister to the congregation here—and why such labours abundant? So that, in the mercy of a compassionate Saviour, and by the power of an Almighty God, I may in the will of God have a prosperous journey to come unto you again: for I long to see you, that I may impart unto you some spiritual gift. Beloved daughter, pray for me, and for this same thing to be prospered of God. Amen and amen.

The grace of our Lord Jesus Christ be with thy spirit.

My love continues ever with your every step, in spirit never having left your company, by the grace of him who saith, 'I will never leave thee, nor forsake thee'. By whom I echo, Nor shall his slave leave thee, nor forsake thee. Amen.

John Metcalfe

John Metcalfe Publishing Trust,
Church Road, Tylers Green,
Penn, Buckinghamshire.

Miss Sie Siok Hui,
Singapore 1024.   8.3.85

John Metcalfe, a servant of God, and slave of Jesus Christ, to my dear daughter in the faith:
Grace, mercy, and peace be to thee, from God our Father and the Lord Jesus Christ.

I AM writing briefly in answer to your letter, but, of course, since then you telephoned me and we spoke together, although we appeared to have been cut off at the end of the call. My dear Siok Hui, it grieves me greatly to hear the distress in your voice, and the trials through which you are passing, and I feel so deeply for you, as, indeed, I do for Lai Yok and Sook Keng also.

I have written at length what I consider to be the path of wisdom for you all in a letter to sister Puni, which should be with you in a week or so from now: I do hope you are able to encourage one another, and that my letters to each are a help to all. It is very important that you attend to what I have said to sister Puni.

Please do not be too harsh in your criticism either of the work in yourself, or in others. Although the system you have left is contrary to the word of God, as was the far greater part of its doctrine, nevertheless many truly cried to God, and by his grace were answered, and, if not established in the truth, yet in themselves were comforted and blessed.

Although all this was a matter of inward feelings, rather than on a basis of the doctrine of the gospel, notwithstanding, it was a real work of grace, and if those that were Christ's knew not the foundation, he did, and he founded them upon it. What was lacking was their knowledge of it. That knowledge, you felt and sensed in the gospel of grace when I came among you. But God had favoured you before: that is why you responded so readily and whole-heartedly.

You have absolutely rightly left the unscriptural system. Nevertheless, the God that heard your cries then and answered them then, despite the system, is still with you, and always will be: This God is our God for ever, he will be our guide even unto death.

In leaving what is wrong, remember, your prayers when in it were not wrong, and, above all, nor were his answers: now you see there is more, doubt not his blessing to you then, nor his leading you out to the promised rest. Trust thou in him. Doubt dishonours him. Faithlessness discredits Christ.

Be at peace as to the Lord hearing prayer and having answered your cries heretofore. Then, pray, believing, for the future. He cannot fail: he cannot deny himself.

Pray for me, my daughter.

Grace be with thee, and all my love in Christ,

John Metcalfe

John Metcalfe Publishing Trust,
Church Road, Tylers Green,
Penn, Buckinghamshire.

Miss Sie Siok Hui,
Singapore 1024.   21.3.85

John Metcalfe, an elder, and a slave of Jesus Christ, to Siok Hui, my dearly beloved daughter in Christ: Grace be to thee, mercy, and peace, from God our Father and the Lord Jesus Christ.

I CANNOT refrain from expressing my joy at your letter of the 12th of this month. This has brought great comfort and consolation to me, and I rejoice with thanksgiving to read of your more settled and trusting frame of heart and mind. This is my daughter indeed!

This is following me as I follow Christ. And because of it, I will tell you a secret: in all the time I was in Malaysia and Singapore, I suffered great affliction and travail of spirit, at times so profound that I could hardly bear the burden pressing upon me: but I would never suffer another to know of it, lest I should be the means of discouraging the sheep for whom Christ died. 'If I say, I will speak thus; behold, I should offend against the generation of thy children.' But that my children tell me only of their sorrows, is both good and right.

Besides, how else should we prove the infallible certainty of his faithfulness who said, 'But thou, when thou prayest, enter into thy closet, and when thou hast shut thy door,

126

pray to thy Father which is in secret; and thy Father which seeth in secret shall reward thee openly.' But this, we have proved abundantly, over and over again, and, as to my travail among you, behold, 'As soon as Zion travailed, she brought forth'! and so I have proved it to be, to the glory of God the Father, through Jesus Christ our Lord.

Nevertheless, the corn of wheat must fall into the ground, and die. And who would wish otherwise, seeing that we follow such a wonderful Saviour and Lord, and earnestly desire that he should see of the travail of his soul, and be satisfied.

Now then, my dear daughter must pardon the shortness of this letter: only, I am so pleased with you, that I must write these few lines of thanksgiving and praise.

The Lord bless you so much the more, Siok Hui, as it is written, Blessed be thou of the Lord, my daughter.

One last thing: In a letter to Lai Yok, I asked her to send me photographs of those for whom she requested prayer, including herself. You remember, this was John Sung's excellent practice, and he laboured much in prayer on this account. Could you do the same for me, and send me a small photograph of yourself and others you wish me to pray for, giving me the names clearly? I hope this will not conflict with what I asked Mary to do, but it would be profitable for me.

Now, keep praying, and be renewed by his Spirit in the inner man in assurance and confidence through the

power and glory of Christ, to grant our desire for a great
door and effectual to be opened in Singapore. Amen.

My pure and fervent love
to my beloved daughter in Christ,

John Metcalfe

John Metcalfe Publishing Trust,
Church Road, Tylers Green,
Penn, Buckinghamshire.

Miss Sie Siok Hui,
Singapore 1024.   2.5.85

John Metcalfe, an elder, and a slave of Jesus Christ,
to Sie Siok Hui, my daughter in Christ, who liketh well to
sit in misery and commiserate with herself, or any who
will listen, running away from the truth of the love of
Christ, and the glorious gospel of the blessed God, lest
being taken up with HIM leave her too little time to
continue with her self-preoccupation; nevertheless,
Grace, mercy, and peace, from God our Father and the
Lord Jesus Christ, the Son of the Father, in truth and love.

STRAIGHTWAY my daughter overturns the counsel
of the Lord: told that 'the less one thinks of self, the

more one thinks of the glory of God, the better', she darkens counsel without knowledge and wails, But what is the glory of God? and goes on to what she thought it was when beguiled in the JSM, and, Woe is her, she is undone; Oh, alas, O, saith she, woe is me, I have no idea what the glory of God is, Oh, Oh, my poor state: and back she goes to her mirror.

But we, beholding as in a glass the glory of the Lord— not our own faces, neither our own self—are changed from glory to glory into the same image! What is the glory of God? The God of glory appeared unto Abraham, when he began to reveal himself, and what appeared? Did Abraham's sin, misery, condemnation, failure, 'problems', or any suchlike self-centred thing appear? No: what appeared was that GOD JUSTIFIETH THE UNGODLY BY FAITH.

No doubt but that Abraham well knew his own corruption. No doubt but he knew the filth of the flesh. No doubt but he knew the power of evil, and the strength of the accuser. No doubt but he knew the king of terrors, the sorrows of death, the pains of hell, the depths of despair, and that pit wherein is neither bottom nor sides, out of which seemeth no escape.

And no doubt he knew all these things infinitely more than my daughter knows them: besides all the disadvantages she thinks she has: Oh, far worse off was this lonely pilgrim. No doubt but that he knew all these things, for 'an horror of great darkness fell upon Abram'.

But, knowing them, he did not try to reform himself, make the flesh better, nor attempt a kind of holiness to appease the Almighty, or self-improvement to bring in the great God as his supposed debtor: No, he earnestly, thoroughly, utterly, and completely owned up his state, confessed it, showed it, brought it as it was to the light, knowing in his conscience he deserved wrath and condemnation, but falling before the LORD for mercy, for grace, for pardon, that God himself might take his case in hand.

And God did take his case in hand, who did no work, who 'worketh not, but believeth on him that justifieth the ungodly', who, self-abhorred and self-judged, cast himself wholly on his mercy, and what? Why, his faith was counted for righteousness.

Now it was not written for his sake alone, that it, righteousness, was counted or imputed to him. That is, a righteousness that he had not wrought, for he could not work, but a righteousness GOD WROUGHT FOR HIM BY THE BLOOD OF CHRIST; no, it was not written for his sake alone, but for Sie Siok Hui's sake also, who believeth, and cannot, dare not deny, that she believeth on him that raised up Jesus our Lord from the dead; who was delivered for our offences, and raised again for our justification. HER JUSTIFICATION. That is, for my daughter's BEING ACCOUNTED RIGHTEOUS IN THE SIGHT OF GOD BECAUSE OF THE BLOOD OF JESUS SHED FOR ALL SHE IS, AND ALL THAT SHE HAS DONE, IS DOING, OR EVER SHALL DO. Do you hear that, girl?

I am sent to preach deliverance to the captive, and delivered you shall be. Oh, say you, alas, woe is me, Oh, I am undone, woe, woe is me. Oh, say I, and why is that? My state, my state, how can he look upon me?

Was that Abraham's language? And was his state not worse? But what saith the scripture? He believed God—in what he would do by the blood of Christ—and it was accounted to him for righteousness. But my STATE, moans Siok Hui, Alas, my state. But GOD'S GLORY, cries John Metcalfe, Glory, his glory! Woe, woe, woe, alas, alack, bewails Siok Hui, I am undone, I know not what is his glory. His glory, say I, IS TO JUSTIFY THE UNGODLY THROUGH THE COMPLETE SUBSTITUTIONARY SACRIFICE OF THE SON OF MAN IN THEIR PLACE.

Then, saith Sie Siok Hui, If it be so, why am I thus? Why art thou thus, pursueth her father in the spirit of prophecy, which is the testimony of Jesus, Why art thou thus? Because thou dishonourest God by setting things on their head, and putting error for truth, and light for darkness, so that thou mayest indulge thy self-pity at the expense of his love and truth.

Oh, what a maudlin picture you have portrayed of yourself, in the picture gallery of your heart. What a picture gallery! Every portrait is of Sie Siok Hui, and the poor, misunderstood waif sadly going from exhibit to exhibit on an endless round, is Sie Siok Hui, herself. And, saith she, till the pictures improve, till the sad waif is joyful, I will not believe. Oh? Except thou put thy finger in the nail-print in his hands, and thrust thy hand into his side, thou wilt not believe? Blessed are they that have not seen, but believe.

Then what is it? Till you find yourself in a better state, you will NOT OWN THE WORK OF GOD ON YOUR BEHALF IN

JUSTIFYING YOU BY BLOOD IN CHRIST YOUR SUBSTITUTE. This is to attempt to justify yourself by works, and lies at the heart of your misery and unbelief. But, Abraham believed God, who justifieth THE UNGODLY, and it was counted to him for righteousness.

Thus he obtained peace and deliverance, and thus will you, and so it shall come to pass ere many days pass, or the Lord hath not sent me. But still you cry, What of my state? I answer, YOUR STATE WAS CRUCIFIED. But what of my misery, my sinfulness, my waywardness, my peevish, sullen, perverse spirit? What of it? HE BARE OUR SINS IN HIS OWN BODY ON THE TREE. And, in consequence, saith he, Their sins and their iniquities will I remember no more.

But ought I not to be holy, cries Siok Hui? Yes, but only as it flows from joyful gratitude FOR HAVING BEEN JUSTIFIED BY GRACE THROUGH FAITH beforehand. So I pursue my daughter, driving her out of her secret hiding-places, holding forth the word of life from which she runs without success. Nor will you ever have any more success than Jonah. For I wot well that whom God blesseth, IS blessed; and not because of themselves, but despite themselves. And moreover, I say unto thee, Blessed art thou of the LORD, my daughter.

Now, as to holiness, that is, putting away the flesh, and joying and dwelling in the Spirit, when did this happen to Abraham, before or after justification? If before, then he was justified by works, and the reward could not be reckoned of grace, but debt. By his holy self-improvement he would have earned it. But did he? No, for the scripture calls him, whilst actually being justified, UNGODLY! Then grace is unearned, unmerited, and free, and only those that know and feel their UNGODLINESS are children to Abraham, and able to be justified. But your ungodliness is just what you do feel, Siok Hui.

Now, after Abraham WAS justified, had peace with God, and rested in his love, then, then, THEN, he was circumcised. That is, then the flesh was removed by the faith of the operation of God. Not to be justified, but because he was justified.

God's glory is to justify sinners, my daughter, that is God's glory. And you hath he justified. Therefore, the less one looks at self, and the more at the glory of God, the better. Wherefore, I say unto thee, 'LOOK AND LIVE'. Amen.

From a truly loving father,

to his well-beloved daughter,

John Metcalfe

John Metcalfe Publishing Trust,
Church Road, Tylers Green,
Penn, Buckinghamshire.

Miss Sie Siok Hui,
Singapore 1024.   21.5.85

John Metcalfe, a servant of God, and of the Lord Jesus
Christ, to Siok Hui, my own daughter in the faith:
Grace, mercy, and peace, from God our Father and the
Lord Jesus Christ.

I HAVE kept your letter of the 29th of the fourth month
on my desk, and although you tell me not to bother
to reply, I assure you that it is not a bother, but a pleasure,
for you are all written on my heart, to live and to die
with you.

Surely this is the work of God, the work of the en-
graver, Exodus 28:9-11,21,36, in which the engraving
upon the head, shoulders, and heart, was not something
that Aaron did, but which the LORD commanded Moses
to be done to Aaron, as his garments signified. This of
course is fulfilled spiritually in Christ our High Priest, in
that we are not in his outward garments, but graven in
his very thoughts, responsibilities, hands, and heart for
ever, and that, as given him of his Father: 'Thine they
were, and thou gavest them me.'

This is reflected in Christ's present ministry from glory,
and felt therefore in the hearts of his servants. II Corin-
thians 3:2, 'Ye are our epistle written in our hearts.' And
who wrote that epistle? The apostles? No, for Paul declares
that this interior epistle, of beloved persons and names,
was written, not that he wrote it. Nor that they wrote it,

whose names were inscribed, but, verse 3, that it was 'the epistle of Christ'. Then, Christ wrote it, and wrote it where no outward pen could ever reach, namely in the heart. That is, the hearts of his true servants whom he sends.

Now then, if you are all so written in my heart, I ask you to consider, Who wrote it? If Christ, then, must he not love you? And if he loves you, shall he not love you to the end? 'Jesus, having loved his own which were in the world, he loved them unto the end.' For this love is strong as death, yea, death hath no power over it, death is but a ditch over which this love strides, from time to eternity, from this world to the next, bearing all those whom he thus loves in its everlasting arms.

This writing on my heart, therefore, is greatly for your encouragement, and shows not what you have done for him, but what he has done for you. Not what you feel for him, but what he feels for you. Not what you are to work for him, but what he has accomplished, and shall assuredly yet accomplish for you. Praise the Lord!

So it is no hardship for me to write. Always you are upon my heart. Moreover, I am very conscious of your present conflicts and trials in the flesh, and how they cross your nature, but none the less, which, if endured, will bring great profit, and will reveal what otherwise you cannot know. Trust in the Lord, for he shall surely bring it to pass. Be strong, and of a good courage.

Indeed, now is the time for you to forget yourself—for how self-centred our nature is found out to be!—and really take up the LORD's interests: and, I truly believe, this is to pray with renewed vigour, faith, and importunity for my return. There are many adversaries, and many difficulties, and there have been many things put in the way:

but over all of these reigns Jesus Christ our Lord, the Son of God, and we are greatly to honour him by making petition to him, and through him to God and the Father, both in the closet, together with others most like-minded, and also in the meetings for prayer.

I believe that all the smaller difficulties, all the lesser and more personal petitions, including your own, will find their answer in the answer to this great heart-yearning and hungering prayer for the preaching of the gospel of God concerning his Son to be given an entrance, and free course, in Singapore. Here is the blessing that carries with it every blessing. Therefore, 'Brethren, pray for us'. And, says Paul, 'For me, that the word of the Lord may have free course.'

Set your affections on things above, where Christ is, Siok Hui, and be assured of the only love that never fails, for youth and old age, time and eternity, this world and the next, even the love of God which is in Christ Jesus our Lord.

And, I repeat, pray earnestly for me. This I beg of my dear daughter: do not fail me.

With my continued care and affection in Christ Jesus,

John Metcalfe

Sie Siok Hui

Temple Orchard,
High Wycombe,
Buckinghamshire.

Miss Sie Siok Hui,
Singapore 1024.   2.9.86

My dearest Siok Hui,

I AM writing to you because I have written to Choon Fah, and I know you will think, What about me?

What about you? You are loved with everlasting love. The love of God from eternity was set upon you, the love of the Father reached in Christ from everlasting into a time not in existence, into a world not created, to a creature not formed, and assuredly and certainly made choice of her from the endless ages before the world was, to show forth in her what GRACE is, what MERCY is, and what a VESSEL OF MERCY such a poor, weak, helpless being should prove to be in time, because of nothing but free, sovereign, distinguishing, redeeming, electing grace.

Oh, cry, Grace, grace unto it, my beloved daughter, it is nothing of self, nothing of you, nothing in you can prevent it, it is all of grace, and all for God's glory, 'to the praise of the glory of his grace'.

What of you? You are loved by the love of Jesus on the cross at Golgotha, all your filth, your uncleanness, your iniquity, were poured into the Substitute, all the real trespasses and actual transgressions, from birth to death, all the state in Adam, was transferred, all, all, all was transferred, to the Substitute upon the tree. 'He hath *made*

137

him to be sin for us.' Then, all God's wrath, all his waves, all his billows, all his everlasting anger, were swallowed up by our Saviour. Oh praise the Lord, let us exalt his name together, beloved daughter, praise ye the Lord.

What of you? You shall be kept, your sins shall not prevail, your worldliness shall not prevail, your unbelief shall not prevail, your deadness shall not prevail, nothing shall prevail against the love of God which is in Christ Jesus our Lord.

He will and you shall. It is impossible that the Spirit and providence of God can fail to bring in every last one for whom Christ died. Poor love, you say, but did he die for me? He surely did. Self-condemned, doubting, sometimes despairing, often hardening: but how do you know these states without Christ? All these are marks of the sheep for whom Christ died! But you know you love him. You think not? Then you know you love his people, and certainly his ministers. Deny that if you can. And you know you would give everything for one look from his eyes, which ravish your heart.

With all my love, my dearest sister,

John Metcalfe

138

John Metcalfe Publishing Trust,
Church Road, Tylers Green,
Penn, Buckinghamshire.

Miss Sie Siok Hui,
Singapore 1024.   18.11.87

My daughter,

SEEK I not rest for thee, that it may be well with thee?
You cannot believe that he can still love you, but I believe.

You cannot believe because you see how foul, how filthy, you are, an unclean fountain either dormant, when your mind is taken with worldly trifles and frivolous talk, or active, when a disgusting fountain bubbles up its unspeakable filth, when you are overcome with remorse and despair. How can he love you?

Did he ever love you? You thought so, once in a while. But now you see this irremediable fountain of iniquity has broken out, you have offended against the generation of his children, and you know he cannot love you. Oh? Could he not see that years ago, though you were blind to it? Have you discovered now what you suppose was hidden then to the eye of the All-seeing, that you think he can only see with your eyesight? He saw it all from the first, yea, before thou camest forth from the womb.

'I have loved thee with an everlasting love.' When did that start? Could he not see everything from eternity, that your blind eyes only begin to discover now? When will that love end, which is called everlasting? When you think yourself unfit, at some point or other?

But you wallow in self-pity. Yes you do. But you are so fickle. Yes you are. But worldliness is present with you. Yes it is. But filth, awful filth, fills and stains your inside so foully and so constantly. Yes it does. And yet you are proud. Yes. Imperious. Yes. Haughty. True. But your state is incorrigible, impossible, it only gets worse. Yes, it does. But it can get nothing but worse, filthier, more truculent, more despairing, more hopeless. Quite so. This is called the flesh. It cannot get better. It cannot be improved. It can only get more corrupt. That is why Jesus bore it into judgment at the tree.

But we must live with it. Or rather, reckon ourselves dead to it. You are no different from me, from any of us. But you make more of a fuss, you want to draw attention to yourself, you want to be noticed, in a word, you give in to pride. So what? Did he not see that when he loved you from everlasting? Does that alter everlasting love glorified with five scars over your very head at this moment as you read? The scars are read by God, even as these words are read by you. You read 'read by you'. He reads 'Siok Hui was judicially crucified, all the filth, all of it, borne by the great Lover of her soul.' Read with him, Siok Hui, bow the neck, read with him.

Go quietly, my daughter, go quietly. Seek I not rest for thee? Daughter, go in peace, thy sins be forgiven thee. This is the whisper of heaven. The old man, the corrupt flesh, its filthy fountain, changed not, though judged once in Christ. But the Spirit will help you, he will comfort you, he will support you. Come down now, my daughter, come down to where I am, in the dust, nothing, but if nothing, abiding in the place of hope, nor letting false pride keep me out. Join me? Or rather, join us with him.

140

Humble yourself, seek nothing, no name, no place for yourself, but be humble, come to Penang with those who love you. 'And Ruth said, Intreat me not to leave thee, or to return from following after thee: for whither thou goest, I will go; and where thou lodgest, I will lodge: thy people shall be my people, and thy God my God: where thou diest, will I die, and there will I be buried: the LORD do so to me, and more also, if ought but death part thee and me.'

Unite, my dear daughter, fear not. Be not afraid of all your fears. Come with us to his feet, and all else will solve itself. Have not I told thee? Your heart may be too bruised and hurt to feel much. No matter. Your soul too torn and perplexed to hope or see or even trust. No matter. It may be too dark to know where to put one step. Never mind. Put your hand in his: it is there. He will not let you fall. Have not I told thee? Come back now, gently, humbly. Come home, my poor, dear, tempestuous, fickle, but blood-bought child. Do let me see your face at Penang: I will not intrude, nor suffer others to disturb my daughter. Be humble: be patient. Thou shalt surely joy again in the LORD. Now reach out and take his hand.

Would I write this, had I no command? Saith not the voice of the Lord Jesus, Seek I not rest for thee, that it may be well with thee?

John Metcalfe

YEO CHEUNG GHEEM

THE TESTIMONY OF
Yeo Cheung Gheem

Singapore,

26.7.89.

Dear Mr. Metcalfe,

THANK you so much for the word of God preached in Penang. We are hearing the tapes again and they seem even more clear than when first heard. In fact, each time when I hear the tapes again, they are so much more powerful and so refreshing.

My heart truly rejoices in the marvellous works of God. Though unworthy as I am, I am very grateful to be brought into the way of the ancient landmarks by which our fathers were led and according to which they first trod —to be shown those ancient pathways and boundary stones, and to be led into them by his blessed Holy Spirit, this is truly too marvellous in my sight.

As I pondered over the works of God and considered all that he had done in my life, I thought it meet that I should write to you of what God has done for me.

145

I was brought up in a rather staunch Taoist family, in a kampong; whilst there I was educated in a convent. I continued my education in another convent when I shifted out into the new town. It was not until I was in secondary one (about thirteen years old) that I was told about Jesus by some of my friends. A small group of my friends (about three or four young girls) started a sort of bible-study group called a 'cell group'. Those that attended 'church' would sometimes share with us what they had learnt and heard, but most of the time, we spent the time sharing or singing 'hymns'. I was one of those that would attend their meetings after school secretly, not daring to let my parents know.

When I was in secondary two (about fourteen years old) something happened within my family that really shook me up. I can't remember how it happened or why it happened but my mother tried to commit suicide. I remember coming home from school to see my house in a commotion and my mother crying. I was shocked when I learnt what had happened. The children were blamed for the incident on account of being naughty, but I doubt it was this. We were made to kneel before her to ask for forgiveness. Stunned, I just did it. I kept asking myself, Why did my mother want to do such a thing? What would happen if she should die? Where would she go? It just frightened me to think of death.

I remember going to school the next day, confused, and I cried and confided in one of my friends, an Anglican girl, and she told me to accept Jesus as my Saviour, and he will help me. Out of desperateness, I did it and prayed the 'sinner's prayer' as they called it. But after doing that, I felt no change at all, and my problem was still there. I was really miserable.

146

I think I went on like this for some time (I can't re-member how long) until one day I couldn't take it any more. And being left alone that night in the house, I went and bowed down before the Taoist altar with their gods and prayed that if they be the true gods, to tell me. Then I went to the bedroom (which I shared with my parents, sister, and brother) and to my bed, and knelt and prayed to Jesus, that if he were the true God, to tell me and show me the truth. Then I cried till I slept.

Deep within me I knew there was a true God, but I didn't know which one. I didn't attend any 'church' but I did visit the idols' temples sometimes with my parents.

During my secondary school days, I would also attend this 'cell group' regularly. Whenever there was opportun-ity I would find time outside my home to read the bible. I usually sought solace in the catholic chapel, next to my school, during recess times. My first bible was a K.J.V. (Authorized Version) given to me by a Seventh-day Ad-ventist girl. I had difficulty trying to read it because I wasn't used to the older English as I supposed then. I was told to try the Living Bible but instinctively I didn't like it. I was also told to use other versions but because of lack of finance, I had to use my K.J.V. first. Despite the difficulty, I just loved reading the Book of Psalms. Maybe it was because I could see, in some small measure, eye to eye with the experience of the psalmist.

As the years went by, I felt more and more convinced that this Jesus, whom I'd heard and read of, was the true God. I remember reading in one of the psalms about the idols which the heathen worship—having mouths but they spoke not, eyes but saw not, ears but they heard not, noses but smelled not. And I remember feeling within myself how true these things were and how ridiculous that men should bow down to a god made by their own hands! How can it be a god then?

It was not till I was in secondary four (about sixteen years old) that I felt I can't go on denying what I've believed. I felt that since I've embraced Christianity, I ought to confess it and not be a hypocrite. In fact, my conscience very often troubled me when I bowed down before the idols, holding the joss-sticks. I wanted to stop doing it but I found no courage to do so. I really felt so hypocritical.

One day, early in the morning, I was awakened by my mother, to wash myself and go to pray to my 'god' mother (the idol goddess of mercy) as it was 'her' birthday. I tried to avoid it by pretending to sleep but my mother dragged me out of bed.

But I just couldn't do it. I felt a strong prompting within me to make a stand. I felt all strength not to compromise even though my mother had gone from the room. I just couldn't bring myself to hold the joss-sticks and to bow before the idol goddess. I went and told my mother, I don't want to pray to her gods and I don't want to hold the joss-sticks any more.

The fury that lit up in her face was enough to scare the daylights out of me but I marvel at the courage granted unto me to stand at that time. I was literally dragged to the altar and the joss-sticks were thrust before my face as I was told to bow and pray. I refused to do so and wrung free from my mother.

When my mother saw my stubbornness, she called my father and took the cane and said, she will beat me to death. My mother really caned me till she's tired. Then my father shouted and scolded me for daring to change my religion without his approval. In between sobs, I told my father that I'm old enough to decide on my own beliefs. But that answer really blew his top.

Then I was locked up at home and forbidden to go to school any more. My mother told me that they will not allow me to sit for the 'O' levels and no more school for me. I was crying non-stop, but when I heard that, my heart really sank. To me, going to school was like a door of freedom. Within my heart, I told the Lord, I can't take it. To stay at home was like a torture as I knew that every movement that I made would be watched. The thought of not being able to read God's word and to have some time of quietness was utterly heart-breaking.

It happened on a sixth day and the next two days were the week-end, but I was locked in and forbidden to go out at all. I was really miserable.

But thanks be unto God for his compassion and love, for that following second day, my parents relented (to my great surprise) and allowed me to go to school. (I think my grandma talked to them.) I was so glad to be freed.

But when I reached school, I couldn't help but burst out into tears when I thought how short this liberty might be—not knowing what the next day might bring forth. I told one of my friends what had happened and said that I might not be able to see her or them again.

But thanks be unto God, who didn't try me beyond that which I'm able to bear, but did make a way of escape for me. I was allowed to go back to school and to complete my education. I was really very grateful unto God for his kindness.

What really filled my heart with joy, was the fact that after that incident, my parents didn't try to make me to hold the joss-sticks any more nor force me to burn the incense nor demand that I should bow to their idols. I was really glad for the deliverance — because, knowing them, I would have thought that they would force me again the next time, but they didn't. It was just marvellous how the Lord worked.

After the 'O' levels, I went to a catholic junior college. In college, our 'cell group' still continued and as it had grown larger, we felt we ought to get someone to conduct proper bible study. One of my friends, who was the niece of Peter Ng, the founder of the 'Jesus Saves' Mission, recommended a 'JSM' missioner to us.

But despite all these things (the 'cell group' and bible studies) my heart yearned to go to a true 'church'. I felt that it was time that I should attend a 'church'. This yearning and desire was so strong that I felt I must do it despite what it might cost me.

It was not until I was in Pre. U. II (about eighteen years old) that I took courage to do so. I remember that first day morning when I woke up. The desire and fear that was upon my heart, I know not how to express. Brushing aside my fears, I told myself that it was now or never. I quickly got up, washed, had my breakfast, and changed.

I told my mother that I was going to 'church'. My mother told me to go and tell my father and sternly told me not to go, or else. I was quite frightened and I went back to the room and hesitated. But my sister, who heard it, whispered to me to go ahead. When I heard that, I felt I must go, all the more.

I went to the door, but before opening it, I politely told my father and mother that I was going to 'church'. I could feel the immense tension that had built up at that time, waiting to burst forth. I waited a while before I closed the door quietly. While I was about to go down the stairs, my father suddenly opened the door and shouted at me never to come back home again and slammed the door so hard that I could feel as if the whole block shook.

I was shocked. As I walked down the stairs, I couldn't control the tears that kept rolling down from my eyes. I just couldn't believe that my father would drive me out of the house.

Actually, when I went out of the house, I really had no idea which 'church' I should go to. I didn't tell my friends about it nor did I make prior arrangements with them. I don't know why. But I did commit it to God to lead me to the true 'church'. In the end, since I've only the 'Jesus Saves' Mission address, I decided to go to 'JSM'.

The first impression that I had of 'JSM' was of coldness and strangeness. After the 'service', everybody just talked and later dispersed to their own groups. I felt so left out. My heart was so heavy and so disappointed. I asked the Lord whether I've come to the right 'church'. My heart was near breaking and I wished I could talk to someone

151

to ask for counsel but there was none. Though my bible-study teacher was there, I just couldn't bring myself to approach him.

At that moment, I really felt as if all that effort and stand that I'd made, seemed to be wasted. I felt rejected both by God and men. I kept asking God, Why? Why lead me into this place, to feel rejected by them? I felt so confused; not knowing what to do next. It seemed like an irony.

After much thought, I decided to go back home and see how the situation was. If my family refused to open the door or if my father drove me out again, I told the Lord that I would take it as his will and would not return again. But if they opened up and didn't drive me away, then, I'd stay and face the consequences.

When I reached home, I was rather frightened to knock at the door, but, summoning up my courage, I knocked quietly for quite some time. I was about to go off, when my younger brother opened the door for me. As I entered the house, I could feel the tension, coldness, and enmity within, so much so that I wished I had not returned. My parents, especially my father, refused to look at me or talk to me. Later on, my mother brought me to the room and I was scolded and interrogated by both my mother and grandmother. I kept quiet most of the time, not daring to cry in front of them, but my heart was near bursting. I learnt from them that my father had intended to beat me up if I should step into the house again but was persuaded not to do so by them.

After that I was interrogated by my father. The fury that was written on his face was really scary. I just sat there trembling. As he talked, I could sense that he was trying to control his anger. I couldn't remember what he told me but I could remember this that he said to me—that if I should ever regret and turn away from my belief, he'll never forgive me nor acknowledge me as his daughter even if I should beg him. At first I couldn't understand what he was trying to tell me as he is a person who always likes to beat around the bush when talking. His statement seemed so contradictory. Later, I realized that he was actually denying me as his daughter. That was the last statement he made. I was really hurt. I told my father that I will not deny my belief. And he just walked away.

But I remembered this verse in Ps. 27:10 which says that when my father and my mother forsake me, then the LORD will take me up. How true it is and I could feel and see for myself how often the LORD would take me up and cause me not to be cast down, especially when my parents treated me with such contempt and at times literally hatred.

I remember how, after that incident, my father never talked to me, but treated me as if I didn't exist at all. Despite all these things, I still treated my parents with respect as I ought to. I still made drinks for my father each evening (which I usually do) but each time I did it, my father would pour it away, even in front of me. I was really hurt that he should hate me so. Ever since then, I decided not to make drinks for him, not because I wanted to retaliate but because I found it useless. I felt it was better that I should keep a low profile.

But trouble did not end there. In fact, this was the beginning of many new trials. Since I'd made that stand,

I decided to persevere in going to 'church' each first day, though at times, I really dreaded going to 'JSM'. I was quite put off by the coldness of the people and the superficiality. I decided to try other 'churches'. But I didn't like them as they seemed too frivolous and light. Comparing them to 'JSM', I felt that 'JSM' was the more sober and disciplined. But I was miserable there.

One day, while I was walking to college alone, I was so miserable that I cried to God within my heart, for help. I don't want to stop going to 'church', since I've made that stand, for I knew that my parents would then laugh at my fall and I felt God's name is at stake. But I also didn't feel like going to 'JSM', seeing the people there were so strange.

As I was complaining to God, these questions suddenly came to me: What are you actually seeking for? Is it for the fellowship of men? To be seen of and sympathized by men? Or is it to seek the face of God and him only? These questions really shook me up from my self-pity. And, as to what my actual cause of wanting to go to 'church', I was really put to shame to see the deceitfulness of my heart.

Then I told myself to stop complaining and grumbling. If my sole aim and purpose was to seek God and to worship him in the 'church' then why did I worry about how the people treated me? Let them be, but just go and seek God. The peace that filled my heart, when the thoughts of my heart were made known, was really marvellous. I asked the Lord for forgiveness and decided to set my heart to seek his face only.

Yeo Cheung Gheem

My parents never left me alone. After attending 'JSM' for a few months, my parents decided to visit 'JSM' to see what it was. I tried to dissuade them, knowing that they will make a commotion there. I told them that it has got nothing to do with them as it is my faith and belief. But whatever I said fell on deaf ears. It seemed that they almost quarrelled with a certain missioner, when he came and talked to them.

But this visit was not the last but the beginning of many such visits to 'JSM' (even up to when it had closed down). Throughout the six years that I was in 'JSM', my parents would never leave me alone. I was even trailed by them to the meetings. At home, there was no peace either, as I was often scolded and threatened by them.

They even came to the extent of thinking I was possessed with an evil spirit. They would go to the mediums to ask for charm papers. These are burnt and their ashes put into the drinks or food. I was given it without my knowledge. I only found out one day, while I was drinking the water, when I saw some residue of ashes in the cup. I was quite angry with my parents and I approached my mother and told her not to do that again. But I committed these things unto the Lord, knowing that my God is greater than theirs, and that my trust is in him alone. I knew that no 'charm' can harm those that are his.

Throughout all these times, I know that it was the Lord that had kept and preserved me. As I consider all these things, I feel no regret for all that the Lord has brought me through. In fact, I'm very, very grateful for all my trials and I wouldn't want to exchange any of them for anything in this world.

It was not until 1984 that I actually thought upon these things that had come upon my way. It was not something that I'd asked for but it just happened. I felt as if God were preparing me for something but I don't know what it was. Since 'JSM' stresses so much on 'calling', I actually thought, maybe, the Lord is preparing me for so-called 'full-time service'. I didn't tell anyone about that until the latter part of 1984. But when it fell on the missioner's ears, he never let me go, but really hounded me about 'my calling'. I told him I'm not sure and I'm not ready. But he said that I'm trying to run away from God's calling. I was really confused and I felt trapped.

It came to pass at that time that there was a conference on Penang Hill. This was in the twelfth month, 1984, where you were asked to preach. I could only attend the latter part of the conference. Before I went up to Penang, I asked the Lord to show me clearly what his will was, so great was my confusion.

I remember the first message that I heard from you was on 'Justification by Faith' on Rom. 3:28. Though I couldn't really understand it, I just loved that spirit that is in you. The joy that lit up your face as you preached it was so real that I told the Lord that I would like to have that selfsame spirit and that joy that is in you. It was so different from other preaching that I've heard.

Because of your coming to Penang and to Singapore, 'my calling' was temporarily taken off the missioner's mind, for which I was most glad. After that, because of the other incidents that followed, this so-called 'full-time service' was forgotten. I felt this was a providence of God and I'm very grateful for being delivered out of that system of bondage and oppression.

156

It is really amazing how the Lord leads each one of his people and gathers us as one company unto himself. It is like what was preached on Psalm 84 wherein the psalmist set out alone but later found a company with him of which 'every one of them in Zion appeareth before God'.

When I heard the message on Jn. 1:23 on the works of John the Baptist, I couldn't help but feel that these are the preparatory works of God in my heart and in my own experience. Of my own self, I know I wouldn't have chosen this pathway. Neither did I ever think or dream of being brought into this blessed privilege, to be under this true gospel ministry. It is truly nothing but grace and grace alone! How amazing and marvellous is his love! It is just too wonderful for me, seeing what manner of person I am, that God should love me so, and give his only begotten Son, to die on the cross for me.

Truly, what is man that God should take knowledge of him? He has not only wrought forth salvation for me, but even condescended to lead me (who am really nothing, but a stinking body filled with putrifying corruption and filthiness) through this pathway with such love and long-suffering unto such a wealthy place in Christ Jesus. Oh, how really amazing and beyond comprehension!

I am very grateful and thankful unto God for all that he has done in my life. Truly, none teacheth like him! But, I do not wish to dwell nor rest in past experiences and deliverances, for there's still much, much more to learn of Christ. Desiring to be made truly empty of all that pertaineth to the flesh (in all its consciousness and sensitivity) that Christ alone be my all in all. O, that my whole being be taken up for his glory alone!

Mr. Metcalfe, please pray for me. (I know you do but I can't help asking for it.)

Thank you so much for this ministry and for bringing this gospel truth into our midst, despite and in spite of the circumstances of your terrible trials and betrayals at that very time. Thank you for being so longsuffering with us throughout these years and for your constant love.

We are all praying for you and for the going forth of the gospel, desiring to see the truth being brought unto many, many souls and many, many countries.

The Lord be with thee and bless thee.

In His everlasting love,
Cheung Gheem

PASTORAL LETTERS TO
Yeo Cheung Gheem

Temple Orchard,
High Wycombe,
Buckinghamshire.

Miss Yeo Cheung Gheem,
Singapore 2260.   9.10.86

My Dear Cheung Gheem,

THANK you for writing to me. I am glad to hear about your new job. I do hope this may ease your mind and relieve the tension you felt in your previous work.

What are all these things? A morning mist. 'What is your life?', asks James, and answers, 'A vapour'. It appeareth for a little time, and then vanisheth away. Then it is our wisdom to lay hold on eternal life, for that appeareth world without end, it is everlasting, it cannot vanish away. The more you do this, the more the things of this life, body, and world will fade. 'Our light affliction, which is but for a moment, worketh for us a far more exceeding and eternal weight of glory.'

We look at the things which cannot be seen. Your life, your frame, the world, people, the passing of time, these things can be seen. Even your grief, your sorrows, your inward sensations, in a certain sense can be seen. But Christ on high, your Father which is in heaven, the Holy Ghost below, the great day of judgment, the resurrection and the life, the holy city, new Jerusalem, the world to come, the everlasting glory, these things cannot be seen.

Yet it is the unseen things that are real, and it is the seen things which are a delusion. 'While we look not at the things which are seen, but at the things which are not seen: for the things which are seen are temporal; but the things which are not seen are eternal.'

It is a twofold exercise. Don't look: do look. Look not; look at. Both attitudes are complementary, both essential, and both require spiritual discipline. Look not at your aching body: who knows who suffers more, for that matter? Why not look? Because we all suffer in the body. 'We that are in this body do groan.' And that pain is worse than anybody's physical affliction. 'I die daily.' 'I bear in my body the marks of the Lord Jesus.' We all have the sentence of death within ourselves. 'Who shall deliver me from the body of this death?' We are filled with 'a loathsome disease: and there is no soundness in my flesh.' The effect of this heightened awareness of our true bodily state, that it is filled with inbred sin, affects us more painfully than those who have the results of such a condition, actual physical infirmity.

What is our antidote then? Christ is our antidote. 'To depart, and to be with Christ; which is far better.' His coming, who bare our infirmities, is the only true healing, and the only true release, and they who look for it, rise over all infirmity, and become careless and indifferent to what they must endure and suffer here below.

These are the true children of Abraham. They consider not their own body, now dead. They look for a city whose builder and maker is God. They look for a country, that is, an heavenly. These are pilgrims and strangers on the earth, who expect tribulation here, knowing that these afflictions are those to which we are appointed. It is their lot, otherwise, where were the strait gate, the narrow way, the way of the cross? 'Take up thy cross—daily— and follow me.'

Nevertheless, I am glad for your change, if you are pleased, and I do hope that it may provide circumstances that help you to wait on the Lord, to rejoice in the Lord, and again I say, rejoice.

I am glad to hear of your fortitude and strength, and encouraged to know how you have persevered. This is God's work, and he will not forsake the work of his hands.

Soon I will begin to make arrangements to come, if the Lord will. Meanwhile, the LORD reigneth, he sitteth upon the floods, he shall laugh, and who shall let it? Blessed be his holy name, his eyes behold, his eyelids try, the children of men. Endure chastening.

Now may the Lord himself comfort you by all means, and the God of all grace be with you.

My abiding love in Christ, as to a dear daughter.

Grace be with thee,

John Metcalfe

John Metcalfe Publishing Trust,
Church Road, Tylers Green,
Penn, Buckinghamshire.

Miss Yeo Cheung Gheem,
Singapore 2260.   26.1.88

My dear Cheung Gheem,

GRACE be unto thee, mercy, and peace, from God the Father, and from the Lord Jesus Christ, the Son of the Father, in truth and love.

I have no greater joy than to hear that my children walk in truth, as we have received a commandment from the

Yeo Cheung Gheem

Father. This is the commandment, that, as ye have heard from the beginning, ye should walk in it.

Keep in the love of God. The enemy will seek to exploit division where he can find occasion. Beware. Watch. Keep that mortified which rose up in the elder brother, when he saw the rejoicing over the prodigal. Remember the words of the Lord Jesus in answer to Peter's 'Till seven times?'. Nay, but forgive, in the deep inward spirit of it, without suspicions, grudge, or the strange fires of jealousy, until seventy times seven. From the heart.

And I am persuaded of you that you will be careful of these very things, and be an example to all the saints, even as you are, beloved Cheung Gheem. For ye need not that any man teach you, but the anointing which ye have received of him teacheth you all things. But as that anointing witnesseth in me also, so I am moved to say this unto you, being confident of this very thing, that he which hath begun a good work in you, will perform it till the day of Christ.

It is a good thing to give praise unto the Lord. Praise is comely in the upright. You rejoice as a true daughter of Zion, and this, O daughter of Jerusalem, fills my heart with joy. In the Spirit, with timbrel and with the dance, you praise God in truth: and the praise of God redounds to his glory by Jesus Christ.

Your love is of God, fresh, pure, and of that everlasting Spirit. Love is of God. This draws the heart after Christ, even as it is in you this day. I know that you must bear many things, although you do not speak of them, and I am very touched to see how you have grown in grace and in the knowledge of our Lord and Saviour Jesus Christ.

As for me, my heart was broken, and is broken, that we were forced to part, but all things are of God, and there are lessons to learn of him, to show fortitude and courage, compassion and love, uprightness and truth, under the Headship of Christ without the help of man, which the more abounds to his praise. Nevertheless I long for the time when we shall all be together again in the Lord's will. Pray for me, dear Cheung Gheem.

My love in Christ,

John Metcalfe

Temple Orchard,
High Wycombe,
Buckinghamshire.

Miss Yeo Cheung Gheem,
Singapore 1129.   1.11.88

My dear Cheung Gheem,

GRACE be to thee, mercy, and peace, from God our Father and the Lord Jesus Christ.

Yeo Cheung Gheem

Your letter was both spiritual and edifying, and I was touched to know that you have turned your illness to interior profit: 'It is good for me that I have been afflicted; that I might learn thy statutes', Ps. 119:71, and one of these statutes is, 'I know that in me (that is, in my flesh,) dwelleth no good thing'.

Another statute learnt experimentally through affliction is this: 'My sore ran in the night, and ceased not', and the following is like unto it, namely, 'My wounds stink and are corrupt because of my foolishness', Ps. 38:5.

All these things are essential, for, without humility, in which we are brought down to the dust and abased in our own eyes, being made to feel our rottenness, no growth can be realized. But if we are inwardly vile in our own sight; if we are made to realize that in our corruption we could never have to do with a holy God; if we feel that his wrath is gone forth against us, and that the blackness of darkness yawns for ever waiting just the other side of death; if 'fearfulness and trembling are come upon me, and horror hath overwhelmed me', Ps. 55:5, then it is true that we can see eye to eye with the psalmist, 'Blessed is the man whom thou chastenest, O LORD, and teachest him out of thy law', Ps. 94:12.

Yet, in itself, this experimental teaching is not the new testament: it prepares for it. It is not the revelation of Christ, it is preparatory to it. It is divine light on ourselves: the showing us our own true state, its utter hopelessness, its incorrigibility, and its being obnoxious to the wrath of God.

Thus we learn that we need a Substitute. From this chastening we learn experimentally our need of One who took our place wholly, and One who gives us his place entirely. A truly objective Substitute, this alone will do for us, One who became us in the place of judgment and whom we became in the place of glory. This is called 'being accepted in the beloved'.

When we are thus taught of God not only to 'flee for refuge to lay hold upon the hope set before us', but, on the account of the horrible sight of ourselves in the light of God's countenance, the terrible view of his holiness under the law, and the fearful, everlasting wrath certain to us from the curse, I say, taught by these things to look wholly to Christ crucified, then we find rest unto our souls. Keep your face fully, wholly, absolutely upturned to Christ, the source of the light, the Light himself, and you shall be changed into the same image from glory to glory, even as by the Spirit of the Lord.

Do not study your health, or seek to change your circumstances, or pity yourself, or think that his grace is not sufficient. The less you consider yourself, your strength or your health, the more you consider Jesus, his strength, and his salvation, the more transformed, the healthier, and the stronger you will be. Say, 'for to me to live is Christ.'

Take your eyes off yourself, or if you must see yourself, see yourself not in the worldly circumstances of bodily weakness, but in the inward sight of filthy, suppurating corruption, so that you will be constrained, nay, compelled, by such a sight to look up, and 'see no man, save Jesus only'. He is thy health, and thy salvation. Look also for his return: it is nearer than when you first believed.

Besides this, live for the good of those weaker in the faith than yourself, imparting that good thing in you by the grace of Christ to their profit.

Keep yourself in the love of God, looking for the mercy of our Lord Jesus Christ unto eternal life.

Pray for me, Cheung Gheem, even as I cry often in prayer for you.

My fervent love in the Spirit of Christ,

John Metcalfe

INDEX

TO OTHER PUBLICATIONS

i

PSALMS, HYMNS AND SPIRITUAL SONGS

THE PSALMS
OF THE
OLD TESTAMENT

The Psalms of the Old Testament, the result of years of painstaking labour, is an original translation into verse from the Authorised Version, which seeks to present the Psalms in the purest scriptural form possible for singing. Here, for the first time, divine names are rendered as and when they occur in the scripture, the distinction between LORD and Lord has been preserved, and every essential point of doctrine and experience appears with unique perception and fidelity.

The Psalms of the Old Testament is the first part of a trilogy written by John Metcalfe, the second part of which is entitled *Spiritual Songs from the Gospels*, and the last, *The Hymns of the New Testament*. These titles provide unique and accurate metrical versions of passages from the psalms, the gospels and the new testament epistles respectively, and are intended to be used together in the worship of God.

Price £2.50 *(postage extra)*
(hard-case binding, dust-jacket)
Printed, sewn and bound
by the John Metcalfe Publishing Trust
ISBN 0 9506366 7 3

SPIRITUAL SONGS

FROM

THE GOSPELS

The *Spiritual Songs from the Gospels*, the result of years of painstaking labour, is an original translation into verse from the Authorised Version, which seeks to present essential parts of the gospels in the purest scriptural form possible for singing. The careful selection from Matthew, Mark, Luke and John, set forth in metrical verse of the highest integrity, enables the singer to sing 'the word of Christ' as if from the scripture itself, 'richly and in all wisdom'; and, above all, in a way that facilitates worship in song of unprecedented fidelity.

The *Spiritual Songs from the Gospels* is the central part of a trilogy written by John Metcalfe, the first part of which is entitled *The Psalms of the Old Testament*, and the last, *The Hymns of the New Testament*. These titles provide unique and accurate metrical versions of passages from the psalms, the gospels and the new testament epistles respectively, and are intended to be used together in the worship of God.

Price £2.50 *(postage extra)*
(hard-case binding, dust-jacket)
Printed, sewn and bound
by the John Metcalfe Publishing Trust
ISBN 0 9506366 8 1

THE HYMNS

OF THE

NEW TESTAMENT

The *Hymns of the New Testament*, the result of years of painstaking labour, is an original translation into verse from the Authorised Version, which presents essential parts of the new testament epistles in the purest scriptural form possible for singing. The careful selection from the book of Acts to that of Revelation, set forth in metrical verse of the highest integrity, enables the singer to sing 'the word of Christ' as if from the scripture itself, 'richly and in all wisdom'; and, above all, in a way that facilitates worship in song of unprecedented fidelity.

The *Hymns of the New Testament* is the last part of a trilogy written by John Metcalfe, the first part of which is entitled *The Psalms of the Old Testament*, and the next, *Spiritual Songs from the Gospels*. These titles provide unique and accurate metrical versions of passages from the psalms, the gospels and the new testament epistles respectively, and are intended to be used together in the worship of God.

Price £2.50 *(postage extra)*
(hard-case binding, dust-jacket)
Printed, sewn and bound
by the John Metcalfe Publishing Trust
ISBN 0 9506366 9 X

'THE APOSTOLIC FOUNDATION
OF THE
CHRISTIAN CHURCH' SERIES

Third Printing

FOUNDATIONS UNCOVERED

THE APOSTOLIC FOUNDATION
OF THE
CHRISTIAN CHURCH

Volume I

Foundations Uncovered is the introduction to the major series: 'The Apostolic Foundation of the Christian Church'.

Rich in truth, the Introduction deals comprehensively with the foundation of the apostolic faith under the descriptive titles: The Word, The Doctrine, The Truth, The Gospel, The Faith, The New Testament, and The Foundation.

The contents of the book reveal: The Fact of the Foundation; The Foundation Uncovered; What the Foundation is not; How the Foundation is Described; and, Being Built upon the Foundation.

'This book comes with the freshness of a new Reformation.'

Price 75p *(postage extra)*
(Laminated cover)
Printed, sewn and bound
by the John Metcalfe Publishing Trust
ISBN 0 9506366 5 7

Thoroughly revised and extensively rewritten
second edition

Third Printing

THE BIRTH OF JESUS CHRIST

THE APOSTOLIC FOUNDATION
OF THE
CHRISTIAN CHURCH

Volume II

'The very spirit of adoration and worship rings through the pages of The Birth of Jesus Christ.

'The author expresses with great clarity the truths revealed to him in his study of holy scriptures at depth. We are presented here with a totally lofty view of the Incarnation.

'John Metcalfe is to be classed amongst the foremost expositors of our age; and his writings have about them that quality of timelessness that makes me sure they will one day take their place among the heritage of truly great Christian works.'

From a review by Rev. David Catterson.

'Uncompromisingly faithful to scripture ... has much to offer which is worth serious consideration ... deeply moving.'

The Expository Times.

Price 95p (postage extra)
(Laminated Cover)
Printed, sewn and bound
by the John Metcalfe Publishing Trust
ISBN 1 870039 48 3

Thoroughly revised and extensively rewritten
second edition (Hardback)

Third Printing

THE MESSIAH

THE APOSTOLIC FOUNDATION
OF THE
CHRISTIAN CHURCH

Volume III

The Messiah is a spiritually penetrating and entirely original
exposition of Matthew chapter one to chapter seven from the
trenchant pen of John Metcalfe.

Matthew Chapters One to Seven

GENEALOGY · BIRTH · STAR OF BETHLEHEM
HEROD · FLIGHT TO EGYPT · NAZARETH
JOHN THE BAPTIST · THE BAPTIST'S MINISTRY
JESUS' BAPTISM · ALL RIGHTEOUSNESS FULFILLED
HEAVEN OPENED · THE SPIRIT'S DESCENT
THE TEMPTATION OF JESUS IN THE WILDERNESS
JESUS' MANIFESTATION · THE CALLING · THE TRUE DISCIPLES
THE BEATITUDES · THE SERMON ON THE MOUNT

'Something of the fire of the ancient Hebrew prophet ....
Metcalfe has spiritual and expository potentials of a high order.'
The Life of Faith.

Price £7.75 *(postage extra)*
Hardback 420 pages
Laminated bookjacket
Printed, sewn and bound
by the John Metcalfe Publishing Trust
ISBN 1 870039 51 3

Second Edition (Hardback)

THE SON OF GOD AND SEED OF DAVID

THE APOSTOLIC FOUNDATION
OF THE
CHRISTIAN CHURCH

Volume IV

The Son of God and Seed of David is the fourth volume in the major work entitled 'The Apostolic Foundation of the Christian Church.'

'The author proceeds to open and allege that Jesus Christ is and ever was *The Son of God*. This greatest of subjects, this most profound of all mysteries, is handled with reverence and with outstanding perception.

'The second part considers *The Seed of David*. What is meant precisely by 'the seed'? And why 'of David'? With prophetic insight the author expounds these essential verities.'

Price £6.95 *(postage extra)*
Hardback 250 pages
Laminated bookjacket
Printed, sewn and bound
by the John Metcalfe Publishing Trust
ISBN 1 870039 16 5

CHRIST CRUCIFIED

THE APOSTOLIC FOUNDATION
OF THE
CHRISTIAN CHURCH

Volume V

Christ Crucified the definitive work on the crucifixion, the blood, and the cross of Jesus Christ.

The crucifixion of Jesus Christ witnessed in the Gospels: the gospel according to Matthew; Mark; Luke; John.

The blood of Jesus Christ declared in the Epistles: the shed blood; the blood of purchase; redemption through his blood; the blood of sprinkling; the blood of the covenant.

The doctrine of the cross revealed in the apostolic foundation of the Christian church: the doctrine of the cross; the cross and the body of sin; the cross and the carnal mind; the cross and the law; the offence of the cross; the cross of our Lord Jesus Christ.

Price £6.95 *(postage extra)*
Hardback 300 pages
Laminated bookjacket
Printed, sewn and bound
by the John Metcalfe Publishing Trust
ISBN 1 870039 08 4

JUSTIFICATION BY FAITH

THE APOSTOLIC FOUNDATION
OF THE
CHRISTIAN CHURCH

Volume VI

THE HEART OF THE GOSPEL · THE FOUNDATION OF THE CHURCH
THE ISSUE OF ETERNITY
CLEARLY, ORIGINALLY AND POWERFULLY OPENED

The basis · The righteousness of the law
The righteousness of God · The atonement · Justification
Traditional views considered · Righteousness imputed to faith
Faith counted for righteousness · Justification by Faith

'And it came to pass, when Jesus had ended these sayings, the people were astonished at his doctrine: for he taught them as one having authority, and not as the scribes.' Matthew 7:28,29.

Price £7.50 *(postage extra)*
Hardback 375 pages
Laminated bookjacket
Printed, sewn and bound
by the John Metcalfe Publishing Trust
ISBN 1870039 11 4

THE CHURCH: WHAT IS IT?

THE APOSTOLIC FOUNDATION
OF THE
CHRISTIAN CHURCH

Volume VII

The answer to this question proceeds first from the lips of Jesus himself, Mt. 16:18, later to be expounded by the words of the apostles whom he sent.

Neither fear of man nor favour from the world remotely affect the answer.

Here is the truth, the whole truth, and nothing but the truth.

The complete originality, the vast range, and the total fearlessness of this book command the attention in a way that is unique.

Read this book: you will never read another like it.

Outspokenly devastating yet devastatingly constructive.

Price £7.75 (*postage extra*)
Hardback 400 pages
Laminated bookjacket
Printed, sewn and bound
by the John Metcalfe Publishing Trust
ISBN 1 870039 23 8

OTHER TITLES

NOAH AND THE FLOOD

Noah and the Flood expounds with vital urgency the man and the message that heralded the end of the old world. The description of the flood itself is vividly realistic. The whole work has an unmistakable ring of authority, and speaks as 'Thus saith the Lord'.

'Mr. Metcalfe makes a skilful use of persuasive eloquence as he challenges the reality of one's profession of faith ... he gives a rousing call to a searching self-examination and evaluation of one's spiritual experience.'

The Monthly Record of the Free Church of Scotland.

Price £1.90 *(postage extra)*
(Laminated Cover)
Printed, sewn and bound
by the John Metcalfe Publishing Trust
ISBN 1 870039 22 X

DIVINE FOOTSTEPS

Divine Footsteps traces the pathway of the feet of the Son of man from the very beginning in the prophetic figures of the true in the old testament through the reality in the new; doing so in a way of experimental spirituality. At the last a glimpse of the coming glory is beheld as his feet are viewed as standing at the latter day upon the earth.

Price 95p *(postage extra)*
(Laminated Cover)
Printed, sewn and bound
by the John Metcalfe Publishing Trust
ISBN 1 870039 21 1

THE RED HEIFER

The Red Heifer was the name given to a sacrifice used by the children of Israel in the Old Testament—as recorded in Numbers 19—in which a heifer was slain and burned. Cedar wood, hyssop and scarlet were cast into the burning, and the ashes were mingled with running water and put in a vessel. It was kept for the children of Israel for a water of separation: it was a purification for sin.

In this unusual book the sacrifice is brought up to date and its relevance to the church today is shown.

Price 75p *(postage extra)*
ISBN 0 9502515 4 2

OF GOD OR MAN?

LIGHT FROM GALATIANS

The Epistle to the Galatians contends for deliverance from the law and from carnal ministry.

The Apostle opens his matter in two ways:

Firstly, Paul vindicates himself and his ministry against those that came not from God above, but from Jerusalem below.

Secondly, he defends the Gospel and evangelical liberty against legal perversions and bondage to the flesh.

Price £1.45 *(postage extra)*
(Laminated Cover)
ISBN 0 9506366 3 0

THE BOOK OF RUTH

The Book of Ruth is set against the farming background of old testament Israel at the time of the Judges, the narrative—unfolding the work of God in redemption—being marked by a series of agricultural events.

These events—the famine; the barley harvest; the wheat harvest; the winnowing—possessed a hidden spiritual significance to that community, but, much more, they speak in figure directly to our own times, as the book reveals.

Equally contemporary appear the characters of Ruth, Naomi, Boaz, and the first kinsman, drawn with spiritual perception greatly to the profit of the reader.

Price £4.95 *(postage extra)*
Hardback 200 pages
Laminated bookjacket
Printed, sewn and bound
by the John Metcalfe Publishing Trust
ISBN 1 870039 17 3

A QUESTION FOR POPE JOHN PAUL II

As a consequence of his many years spent apart in prayer, lonely vigil, and painstaking study of the scripture, John Metcalfe asks a question and looks for an answer from Pope John Paul II.

Price £1.25. *(postage extra)*
(Laminated Cover)
ISBN 0 9506366 4 9

Newly published second edition

Third Printing

THE WELLS OF SALVATION

The Wells of Salvation is written from a series of seven powerful addresses preached at Tylers Green. It is a forthright and experimental exposition of Isaiah 12:3, 'Therefore with joy shall ye draw water out of the wells of salvation.'

John Metcalfe is acknowledged to be perhaps the most gifted expositor and powerful preacher of our day and this is to be seen clearly in The Wells of Salvation.

Price £2.35 *(postage extra)*
(Laminated Cover)
Printed, sewn and bound
by the John Metcalfe Publishing Trust
ISBN 1 870039 72 6

PRESENT-DAY CONVERSIONS
OF THE NEW TESTAMENT KIND

FROM THE MINISTRY OF

JOHN METCALFE

The outstandingly striking presentation of this fascinating paperback will surely catch the eye, as its title and contents will certainly captivate the mind: here is a unique publication.

Woven into a gripping narrative, over twenty-one short life stories, all centred on conversions that simply could not have happened had not God broken in, and had not Christ been revealed, the book presents a tremendous challenge, at once moving and thrilling to the reader.

Price £2.25 (postage extra)
(Laminated Cover)
Printed, sewn and bound
by the John Metcalfe Publishing Trust
ISBN 1 870039 31 9

DIVINE MEDITATIONS

OF

WILLIAM HUNTINGTON

Originally published by Mr. Huntington as a series of letters to J. Jenkins, under the title of 'Contemplations on the God of Israel', the spiritual content of this correspondence has been skilfully and sympathetically edited, abridged, and arranged so as to form a series of meditations, suitable for daily readings.

Mr. Huntington's own text is thereby adapted to speak directly to the reader in a way much more suited to his ministering immediately to ourselves, in our own circumstances and times.

It is greatly hoped that many today will benefit from this adaption which carefully retains both the spirit and the letter of the text. If any prefer the original format, this is readily available from several sources and many libraries.

Nevertheless, the publishers believe the much more readable form into which Mr. Huntington's very words have been adapted will appeal to a far wider audience, for whose comfort and consolation this carefully edited work has been published.

Price £2.35 (*postage extra*)
(Laminated Cover)
Printed, sewn and bound
by the John Metcalfe Publishing Trust
ISBN 1 870039 24 6

SAVING FAITH

The sevenfold work of the Holy Ghost in bringing a sinner to saving faith in Christ opened and enlarged.

True faith is the work of God. False faith is the presumption of man. But where is the difference? *Saving Faith* shows the difference.

Price £2.25 *(postage extra)*
Paperback 250 pages
(Laminated Cover)
Printed, sewn and bound
by the John Metcalfe Publishing Trust
ISBN 1 870039 40 8

DELIVERANCE FROM THE LAW
THE WESTMINSTER CONFESSION EXPLODED

Deliverance from the law. A devastating vindication of the gospel of Christ against the traditions of man.

Price £1.90 *(postage extra)*
Paperback 160 pages
(Laminated Cover)
Printed, sewn and bound
by the John Metcalfe Publishing Trust
ISBN 1 870039 41 6

THE BEATITUDES

A unique insight destined to be the classic opening of this wonderful sequence of utterances from the lips of Jesus.

The reader will discover a penetration of the spiritual heights and divine depths of these peerless words in a way ever fresh and always rewarding though read time and time again.

Price £1.90 *(postage extra)*
Paperback 185 pages
(Laminated cover)
Printed, sewn and bound
by the John Metcalfe Publishing Trust
ISBN 1 870039 45 9

COLOSSIANS

This concise and unique revelation of the Epistle to the Colossians has the hallmark of spiritual originality and insight peculiar to the ministry of John Metcalfe. It is as if a diamond, inert and lifeless in itself, has been divinely cut at great cost, so that every way in which it is turned, the light from above is enhanced and magnified to break forth with divine radiance showing colour and depth hitherto unsuspected.

The Trustees give glory and thanks to God for the privilege of producing and subsidising this work.

Price 95p *(postage extra)*
Paperback 135 pages
(Laminated cover)
Printed, sewn and bound
by the John Metcalfe Publishing Trust
ISBN 1 870039 55 6

PHILIPPIANS

The Epistle of Paul the Apostle to the Philippians is opened by this work from the pen of John Metcalfe with that lucid thoroughness which one has come to expect from a ministry received 'not of men, neither by man, but by the revelation of Jesus Christ'.

The work of God at Philippi is traced 'from the first day' until the time at which the epistle was written. Never were Lydia or the Philippian jailor drawn with more lively insight. The epistle itself is revealed in order, with passages—such as 'the mind that was in Christ Jesus'—that evidence the work of no less than a divine for our own times.

The Trustees give glory and thanks to God for the privilege of producing and subsidising this book.

Price £1.90 *(postage extra)*
Paperback 185 pages
(Laminated cover)
Printed, sewn and bound
by the John Metcalfe Publishing Trust
ISBN 1 870039 56 4

MATTHEW

This concise revelation of the essence and structure of the Gospel according to Matthew, the culmination of years of prayer and devotion, retreat and study, opens the mind of the Spirit in the unique vision of Jesus Christ, the son of David, the son of Abraham, recorded in the first gospel.

The Trustees give glory and thanks to God for the privilege of producing and subsidising this work.

Price 95p *(postage extra)*
Paperback 135 pages
(Laminated Cover)
Printed, sewn and bound
by the John Metcalfe Publishing Trust
ISBN 1 870039 61 0

PHILEMON

This penetrating revelation of the epistle to Philemon opens the substance of four consecutive lectures given by John Metcalfe in The Hoare Memorial Hall, Church House, Westminster, London.

The Trustees give glory and thanks to God for the privilege of producing and subsidising this work.

Price £1.90 *(postage extra)*
Paperback 190 pages
(Laminated Cover)
Printed, sewn and bound
by the John Metcalfe Publishing Trust
ISBN 1 870039 66 1

FIRST TIMOTHY

This penetrating revelation of the first epistle to Timothy opens the substance of five consecutive lectures given by John Metcalfe in The Hoare Memorial Hall, Church House, Westminster, London.

The Trustees give glory and thanks to God for the privilege of producing and subsidising this work.

Price £2.00 *(postage extra)*
Paperback 220 pages
(Laminated Cover)
Printed, sewn and bound
by the John Metcalfe Publishing Trust

ISBN 1 870039 67 X

MARK

This penetrating revelation of the gospel according to to Mark opens the substance of seven consecutive lectures given by John Metcalfe in The Hoare Memorial Hall, Church House, Westminster, London.

The Trustees give glory and thanks to God for the privilege of producing and subsidising this work.

Price £2.35 *(postage extra)*
Paperback 290 pages
(Laminated Cover)
Printed, sewn and bound
by the John Metcalfe Publishing Trust
ISBN 1 870039 70 X

CREATION

This spiritually penetrating and outstandingly original revelation of the Creation opens the substance of five consecutive lectures given by John Metcalfe, commencing in the Hoare Memorial Hall and later moving to the central Assembly Hall, Church House, Westminster, London.

The Trustees give glory and thanks to God for the privilege of producing and subsidising this work.

Price £2.00 *(postage extra)*
Paperback 230 pages
(Laminated Cover)
Printed, sewn and bound
by the John Metcalfe Publishing Trust
ISBN 1 870039 71 8

NEWLY PUBLISHED

PASTORAL LETTERS TO THE FAR EAST

Feeling the abiding spiritual value of letters written by John
Metcalfe in his absence from the Far East, Miss Sie Siok Hui
cherished the correspondence to her, and at the same time
was moved to seek for similar writings to some of her closest
sisters in Christ.

Gathering these letters together, it was her earnest desire that
such an enduring testimony should be made available to all
the faithful remnant in our own day. The result of her prayers
and spiritual exercise appears in the publication 'Pastoral
Letters to the Far East'.

Price £2.00 *(postage extra)*
Paperback 240 pages
(Laminated Cover)
Printed, sewn and bound
by the John Metcalfe Publishing Trust

ISBN 1 870039 74 2

'TRACT FOR THE TIMES' SERIES

'TRACT FOR THE TIMES' SERIES

The Gospel of God by John Metcalfe. No. 1 in the Series. Laminated Cover, price 25p.

The Strait Gate by John Metcalfe. No. 2 in the Series. Laminated Cover, price 25p.

Eternal Sonship and Taylor Brethren by John Metcalfe. No. 3 in the Series. Laminated Cover, price 25p.

Marks of the New Testament Church by John Metcalfe. No. 4 in the Series. Laminated Cover, price 25p.

The Charismatic Delusion by John Metcalfe. No. 5 in the Series. Laminated Cover, price 25p.

Premillennialism Exposed by John Metcalfe. No. 6 in the Series. Laminated Cover, price 25p.

Justification and Peace by John Metcalfe. No. 7 in the Series. Laminated Cover, price 25p.

Faith or Presumption? by John Metcalfe. No. 8 in the Series. Laminated Cover, price 25p.

The Elect Undeceived by John Metcalfe. No. 9 in the Series. Laminated Cover, price 25p.

Justifying Righteousness by John Metcalfe. No. 10 in the Series. Laminated Cover, price 25p.

Righteousness Imputed by John Metcalfe. No. 11 in the Series. Laminated Cover, price 25p.

The Great Deception by John Metcalfe. No. 12 in the Series. Laminated Cover, price 25p.

A Famine in the Land by John Metcalfe. No. 13 in the Series. Laminated Cover, price 25p.

Blood and Water by John Metcalfe. No. 14 in the Series. Laminated Cover, price 25p.

Women Bishops? by John Metcalfe. No. 15 in the Series. Laminated Cover, price 25p.

The Heavenly Vision by John Metcalfe. No. 16 in the Series. Laminated Cover, price 25p.

EVANGELICAL TRACTS

EVANGELICAL TRACTS

1. **The Two Prayers of Elijah.** Green card cover, price 10p.

2. **Wounded for our Transgressions.** Gold card cover, price 10p.

3. **The Blood of Sprinkling.** Red card cover, price 10p.

4. **The Grace of God that brings Salvation.** Blue card cover, price 10p.

5. **The Name of Jesus.** Rose card cover, price 10p.

6. **The Ministry of the New Testament.** Purple card cover, price 10p.

7. **The Death of the Righteous** (*The closing days of J.B. Stoney*) by A.M.S. (his daughter). Ivory card cover, Price 10p.

8. **Repentance.** Sky blue card cover, price 10p.

9. **Legal Deceivers Exposed.** Crimson card cover, price 10p.

10. **Unconditional Salvation.** Green card cover, price 10p.

11. **Religious Merchandise.** Brown card cover, price 10p.

12. **Comfort.** Pink card cover, price 10p.

13. **Peace.** Grey card cover, price 10p.

14. **Eternal Life.** Cobalt card cover, price 10p.

15. **The Handwriting of Ordinances.** Fawn card cover, price 10p.

16. **'Lord, Lord!'.** Emerald card cover, price 10p.

ECCLESIA TRACTS

ECCLESIA TRACTS

The Beginning of the Ecclesia by John Metcalfe. No. 1 in the Series, Sand grain cover, Price 10p.

Churches and the Church by J.N. Darby. Edited. No. 2 in the Series, Sand grain cover, Price 10p.

The Ministers of Christ by John Metcalfe. No. 3 in the Series, Sand grain cover, Price 10p.

The Inward Witness by George Fox. Edited. No. 4 in the Series, Sand grain cover, Price 10p.

The Notion of a Clergyman by J.N. Darby. Edited. No. 5 in the Series, Sand grain cover, Price 10p.

The Servant of the Lord by William Huntington. Edited and Abridged. No. 6 in the Series, Sand grain cover, Price 10p.

One Spirit by William Kelly. Edited. No. 7 in the Series, Sand grain cover, Price 10p.

The Funeral of Arminianism by William Huntington. Edited and Abridged. No. 8 in the Series, Sand grain cover, Price 10p.

One Body by William Kelly. Edited. No. 9 in the Series, Sand grain cover, Price 10p.

False Churches and True by John Metcalfe. No. 10 in the Series, Sand grain cover, Price 10p.

Separation from Evil by J.N. Darby. Edited. No. 11 in the Series, Sand grain cover, Price 10p.

The Remnant by J.B. Stoney. Edited. No. 12 in the Series, Sand grain cover, Price 10p.

The Arminian Skeleton by William Huntington. Edited and Abridged. No. 13 in the Series, Sand grain cover, Price 10p.

FOUNDATION TRACTS

FOUNDATION TRACTS

1. **Female Priests?** by John Metcalfe. Oatmeal cover, price 25p.

2. **The Bondage of the Will** by Martin Luther. Translated and Abridged. Oatmeal cover, price 25p.

3. **Of the Popish Mass** by John Calvin. Translated and Abridged. Oatmeal cover, price 25p.

4. **The Adversary** by John Metcalfe. Oatmeal cover, price 25p.

5. **The Advance of Popery** by J.C. Philpot. Oatmeal cover, price 25p.

6. **Enemies in the Land** by John Metcalfe. Oatmeal cover, price 25p.

7. **An Admonition Concerning Relics** by John Calvin. Oatmeal cover, price 25p.

8. **John Metcalfe's Testimony Against Falsity in Worship** by John Metcalfe. Oatmeal cover, price 25p.

9. **Brethrenism Exposed** by John Metcalfe. Oatmeal cover, price 25p.

10. **John Metcalfe's Testimony Against The Social Gospel** by John Metcalfe. Oatmeal cover, price 25p.

MINISTRY BY JOHN METCALFE

TAPE MINISTRY BY JOHN METCALFE
FROM ENGLAND AND THE FAR EAST
IS AVAILABLE.

In order to obtain this free recorded ministry, please send your blank cassette (C.90) and the cost of the return postage, including your name and address in block capitals, to the John Metcalfe Publishing Trust, Church Road, Tylers Green, Penn, Bucks, HP10 8LN. Tapelists are available on request.

Owing to the increased demand for the tape ministry, we are unable to supply more than two tapes per order, except in the case of meetings for the hearing of tapes, where a special arrangement can be made.

THE MINISTRY OF THE NEW TESTAMENT

The purpose of this substantial A4 gloss paper magazine is to provide spiritual and experimental ministry with sound doctrine which rightly and prophetically divides the Word of Truth.

Readers of our books will already know the high standards of our publications. They can be confident that these pages will maintain that quality, by giving access to enduring ministry from the past, much of which is derived from sources that are virtually unobtainable today, and publishing a living ministry from the present. Selected articles from the following writers have already been included:

ELI ASHDOWN · JOHN BERRIDGE · ABRAHAM BOOTH
JOHN BRADFORD · JOHN BUNYAN · JOHN BURGON
JOHN CALVIN · DONALD CARGILL · JOHN CENNICK · J.N. DARBY
GEORGE FOX · JOHN FOXE · WILLIAM GADSBY · JOHN GUTHRIE
WILLIAM GUTHRIE · GREY HAZLERIGG · WILLIAM HUNTINGTON
WILLIAM KELLY · JOHN KENNEDY · JOHN KERSHAW
JOHN KEYT · HANSERD KNOLLYS · JOHN KNOX · JAMES LEWIS
MARTIN LUTHER · ROBERT MURRAY MCCHEYNE · JOHN METCALFE
THOMAS OXENHAM · ALEXANDER—SANDY—PEDEN · J.C. PHILPOT
J.K. POPHAM · JAMES RENWICK · J.B. STONEY · HENRY TANNER
ARTHUR TRIGGS · JOHN VINALL · JOHN WARBURTON
JOHN WELWOOD · GEORGE WHITEFIELD · J.A. WYLIE

Price £1.75 *(postage included)*
Issued Spring, Summer, Autumn, Winter.

Book Order Form

Please send to the address below:-

	Price	Quantity
A Question for Pope John Paul II	£1.25	......
Of God or Man?	£1.45	......
Noah and the Flood	£1.90	......
Divine Footsteps	£0.95	......
The Red Heifer	£0.75	......
The Wells of Salvation	£2.35	......
The Book of Ruth (Hardback edition)	£4.95	......
Divine Meditations of William Huntington	£2.35	......
Present-Day Conversions of the New Testament Kind	£2.25	......
Saving Faith	£2.25	......
Deliverance from the Law	£1.90	......
The Beatitudes	£1.90	......
Pastoral Letters to the Far East	£2.00	......

Lectures from Church House, Westminster

	Price	Quantity
Colossians	£0.95	......
Philippians	£1.90	......
Matthew	£0.95	......
Philemon	£1.90	......
First Timothy	£2.00	......
Mark	£2.35	......
Creation	£2.00	......

Psalms, Hymns & Spiritual Songs (Hardback edition)

	Price	Quantity
The Psalms of the Old Testament	£2.50	......
Spiritual Songs from the Gospels	£2.50	......
The Hymns of the New Testament	£2.50	......

'Apostolic Foundation of the Christian Church' series

		Price	Quantity
Foundations Uncovered	Vol.I	£0.75	......
The Birth of Jesus Christ	Vol.II	£0.95	......
The Messiah (Hardback edition)	Vol.III	£7.75	......
The Son of God and Seed of David (Hardback edition)	Vol.IV	£6.95	......
Christ Crucified (Hardback edition)	Vol.V	£6.95	......
Justification by Faith (Hardback edition)	Vol.VI	£7.50	..... .
The Church: What is it? (Hardback edition)	Vol.VII	£7.75	......

Name and Address (in block capitals)

. . . .

. . . .

. . . .

If money is sent with order please allow for postage. Please address to:- The John Metcalfe Publishing Trust, Church Road, Tylers Green, Penn, Bucks, HP10 8LN.

Tract Order Form

Please send to the address below:-

Evangelical Tracts		Price	Quantity
The Two Prayers of Elijah		£0.10	......
Wounded for our Transgressions		£0.10	......
The Blood of Sprinkling		£0.10	......
The Grace of God that Brings Salvation		£0.10	......
The Name of Jesus		£0.10	......
The Ministry of the New Testament		£0.10	......
The Death of the Righteous by A.M.S.		£0.10	......
Repentance		£0.10	......
Legal Deceivers Exposed		£0.10	......
Unconditional Salvation		£0.10	......
Religious Merchandise		£0.10	......
Comfort		£0.10	......
Peace		£0.10	......
Eternal Life		£0.10	......
The Handwriting of Ordinances		£0.10	......
'Lord, Lord!'		£0.10	......
'Tract for the Times' series			
The Gospel of God	No.1	£0.25	......
The Strait Gate	No.2	£0.25	......
Eternal Sonship and Taylor Brethren	No.3	£0.25	......
Marks of the New Testament Church	No.4	£0.25	......
The Charismatic Delusion	No.5	£0.25	......
Premillennialism Exposed	No.6	£0.25	......
Justification and Peace	No.7	£0.25	......
Faith or presumption?	No.8	£0.25	......
The Elect undeceived	No.9	£0.25	......
Justifying Righteousness	No.10	£0.25	......
Righteousness Imputed	No.11	£0.25	......
The Great Deception	No.12	£0.25	......
A Famine in the Land	No.13	£0.25	......
Blood and Water	No.14	£0.25	......
Women Bishops?	No.15	£0.25	......
The Heavenly Vision	No.16	£0.25	......

Name and Address (in block capitals)

. . . .

. . . .

. . . .

If money is sent with order please allow for postage. Please address to:- The
John Metcalfe Publishing Trust, Church Road, Tylers Green, Penn, Bucks, HP10 8LN.

Tract Order Form

Please send to the address below:-

		Price	Quantity
Ecclesia Tracts			
The Beginning of the Ecclesia	No.1	£0.10	......
Churches and the Church (J.N.D.)	No.2	£0.10	......
The Ministers of Christ	No.3	£0.10	......
The Inward Witness (G.F.)	No.4	£0.10	......
The Notion of a Clergyman (J.N.D.)	No.5	£0.10	......
The Servant of the Lord (W.H.)	No.6	£0.10	......
One Spirit (W.K.)	No.7	£0.10	......
The Funeral of Arminianism (W.H.)	No.8	£0.10	......
One Body (W.K.)	No.9	£0.10	......
False Churches and True	No.10	£0.10	......
Separation from Evil (J.N.D.)	No.11	£0.10	......
The Remnant (J.B.S.)	No.12	£0.10	......
The Arminian Skeleton (W.H.)	No.13	£0.10	......
Foundation Tracts			
Female Priests?	No.1	£0.25	......
The Bondage of the Will (Martin Luther)	No.2	£0.25	......
Of the Popish Mass (John Calvin)	No.3	£0.25	......
The Adversary	No.4	£0.25	......
The Advance of Popery (J.C. Philpot)	No.5	£0.25	......
Enemies in the Land	No.6	£0.25	......
An Admonition Concerning Relics (John Calvin)	No.7	£0.25	.....
John Metcalfe's Testimony Against Falsity in Worship	No.8	£0.25	......
Brethrenism Exposed	No.9	£0.25	......
John Metcalfe's Testimony Against The Social Gospel	No.10	£0.25	......

Name and Address (in block capitals)

. . . .

. . . .

. . . .

If money is sent with order please allow for postage. Please address to:- The
John Metcalfe Publishing Trust, Church Road, Tylers Green, Penn, Bucks, HP10 8LN.

Magazine Order Form

Name and Address (in block capitals)

. . . .

. . . .

. . . .

Please send me .... current copy/copies of The Ministry of the New Testament.

Please send me .... year/s subscription.

I enclose a cheque/postal order for £ ....

(Price: including postage, U.K. £1.75; Overseas £1.90)
(One year's subscription: Including postage, U.K. £7.00; Overseas £7.60)

Cheques should be made payable to The John Metcalfe Publishing Trust, and for overseas subscribers should be in pounds sterling drawn on a London Bank.

10 or more copies to one address will qualify for a 10% discount

Back numbers from Spring 1986 available.

Please send to The John Metcalfe Publishing Trust, Church Road, Tylers Green, Penn, Bucks, HP10 8LN

All Publications of the Trust are subsidised by the Publishers.